Chasing Masculinity

"Dr. Walker deftly uses social theory and in-depth interviews to explain how social expectations and gender dynamics contribute to the motivations and experiences of men who have affairs. This book will make you rethink your stereotypes about men, and why some 'cheat' on their partners and wives. Sure to be a classic in gender, sexuality and family studies!"

—Arielle Kuperberg, *Associate Professor of Sociology and Women, Gender and Sexuality Studies, UNC Greensboro; Editor-in-Chief of the Council on Contemporary Families Blog @ The Society Pages*

"Why do men cheat? Through interviews with dozens of cheaters, Alicia Walker sets aside assumptions about infidelity and shows that cheating helps men bolster masculinity. By seeking non-marital sexual—and emotional—connections, men reassure themselves that they are desirable and sexually skilled. They interpret cheating as a way to actually preserve their marriages, while ignoring many of the root causes of their relationship problems such as gender inequality. This is a must read for anyone interested in sexuality or gender."

—Tony Silva, *Assistant Professor of Sociology, University of British Columbia*

"This compelling new book challenges many taken-for-granted assumptions about why men cheat and the types of men who cheat. By examining men's motivations to pursue affairs online, Walker highlights the emotional aspects of men's external relationships, revealing that cheating is not just about sex for men. This captivating book thoughtfully considers the complexities of masculinity, intimacy, and infidelity in the digital age, and is highly enjoyable to read."

—Nicole Andrejek, *McMaster University, Research Assistant for the* Sex in Canada *research project*

"In *Chasing Masculinity*, Walker examines the experiences of men in the United States who purposely sought out extramarital relationships on the site Ashley Madison. She challenges our preconceived notions and understandings of why men "cheat." Walker artfully appraises our cultural obsession with infidelity and, by extension, monogamy. She highlights the complexity of negotiating fragile masculinity in often highly sexualized contexts. Memorable quotes and stories allow the reader to question the norms and institutions surrounding romantic relationships. This book is one individuals will talk about long after they finish reading."

—Barbara F. Prince, *Assistant Professor of Sociology, Lebanon Valley College*

"In this book, Walker challenges commonly held assumptions about marital infidelity through a deeply intriguing qualitative exploration of the extramarital experiences of men seeking emotional fulfillment deemed not present in their primary relationships. The rich narrative and unique methodology of *Chasing Masculinity* is guaranteed to boost student engagement and stimulate robust discussion within a variety of course delivery platforms on topics including marriage and family, sex and gender, human sexuality, and research methods."

—Michele Lee Kozimor, *Professor of Sociology, Elizabethtown College; Editor,*
Teaching Sociology

Alicia M. Walker

Chasing Masculinity

Men, Validation, and Infidelity

Alicia M. Walker
Missouri State University
Springfield, MO, USA

ISBN 978-3-030-49817-7   ISBN 978-3-030-49818-4   (eBook)
https://doi.org/10.1007/978-3-030-49818-4

Cover designed by eStudioCalamar

This Palgrave Macmillan imprint is published by the registered company Springer Nature
Switzerland AG
The registered company address is: Gewerbestrasse 11, 6330 Cham, Switzerland

For my beloved son, Alex, my "Big Bird,"
who would have so enjoyed this book,
and whom I will miss the rest of my days

And

to the men of Ashley Madison,
who so richly shared themselves and their experiences with me,
and without whom there would be no book

Acknowledgments

No book is truly written solely by the people listed on the cover. The reality is that it takes a village for a book to come into being. Books are born of stray ideas and long days of staring at blinking cursors as they mock you. And along the way, you need a cheering section. It would be impossible for me to name everyone who contributed to this book, but here are a few of them.

Without Dr. Claire Renzetti's input, this book wouldn't exist. My original vision of the study only included interviewing women, but Dr. Renzetti said, "Go ahead and talk to the men, too. Who knows what you might find?" Indeed, who could've known.

I am forever grateful to Amelia Derkatsch, who reached out to me and saw the potential in this project. Thank you, Palgrave Macmillan, for believing in this book. This manuscript is stronger due to the comments of the reviewers. I cannot thank you enough. I am also grateful to both Poppy Hull and Sharla Plant for stepping in and helping me see this book through to the end. Sharla, you provided much-needed support in those moments of frustration. Additionally, Nina Guttapalle came in with fresh eyes and a fresh perspective to strengthen the book. Thank you for your belief in this work.

My amazingly talented cousin, Dustin Cox, graciously gives his time to read my drafts, help me find the holes in my arguments, and talk me off the ledge when I'm sure the manuscript is irredeemable. With two small children, a full-time job, and the responsibilities of graduate school, his time is precious. Yet he donates it to me anyway. Love you, Cuz!

Social media helps connect us all. To my many friends and family who share my everyday life through *Facebook* and *Twitter,* thank you so much for your positive thoughts, mojo, and good juju. Writing can be so isolating and it's easy to lose hope. You keep me encouraged. Thank you for cheering me on.

The grief of losing my Big Bird is often too large to bear alone. I'm so grateful for my many friends and family, who listen as I talk about my pain and give me a space to think about and remember my sweet boy. It takes strength to face someone else's pain without looking away. I cannot thank you enough. I especially thank my dear friends, Kara Ritthaler, Wiley Loyd, Brandie Gillespie, Kelly Shepard-Hill, Julia Erck, and my cousins, Shannon Cox Fraker, and Tracy Mills, who tirelessly sit with me as I cry and share my loss.

Books command an intense time commitment. Since writers are granted no more time than anyone else, writing time gets stolen from other things in your life, like your family. My family endures the hours I spend writing and rewriting, as well as the hours when I'm preoccupied and thus not as present as I'd like to be. Further, none of my children ever act embarrassed to be the child of a woman who studies sexual topics. In fact, they seem to take some pride in the work I do. My daughter, Avery, listens patiently as I puzzle through my framework. Avery, Mason, and George, I thank you and I love you all. My beloved Alex, you were always so proud of your mother and your endless support kept me afloat. I miss and love you always.

You don't become someone who does the kind of work I do without amazing parents. My mother, Nancy, and my father, Virgil, deeply believed in me and instilled the idea that I could reach for anything I desired and be successful. They taught me so much and made me who I am. My open-mindedness was born at home and nurtured by my parents to whom I owe a tremendous debt of gratitude. Were I not shaped by these two remarkable folks, I couldn't do this work. Thank you.

Last, but certainly not least, I am so thankful for my faithful companion, my rescue dog, Harvey. He has sat at my feet through every word of every draft of this book. Harvey is an excellent writing assistant, who accepts pay in belly rubs and daily walks, which also helped me clear my head. Much of the book is the result of those walks, where I clarified my own argument. Thank you, Harvey! (He doesn't read, but I'll read it to him later.) Adopt, don't shop.

If this book enjoys any success, it is owed to the wonderful folks both listed and not listed here. Thank you.

Contents

About the Author

Alicia M. Walker works as an assistant professor at Missouri State University in the Department of Sociology and Anthropology. As a microsociologist, her work focuses on intimate sexual relationships and behavior, sexualities and sexual identity, and gender. Specifically, her work looks at the social construction of the sexual self, the ways we make sense of ourselves as sexual beings, and the ways we navigate our lived experiences. She has particular interest in closeted sexual behaviors, and is credited with creating a sociology of infidelity. Her work has appeared in *Archives of Sexual Behavior, Sexuality & Culture*, and *Journal of Bisexuality*, among others. Her previous book, *The Secret Life of the Cheating Wife*, investigated women's participation in outside partnerships.

1

The C-Word (Cheater): Infidelity as the Ultimate Threat

We all think we understand men's infidelity. From casual exchanges about celebrity cheating scandals in public spaces to private conversations about the state of our friends' unions to memes on social media, we position ourselves as adultery experts. A popular meme online likens men's cheating to losing a $100 bill to pick up a $1 bill. The original poster, a man, explains that if you had $100 but saw a $1 bill on the floor, you'd pick it up, and then says, "There ya go. That's why boys cheat." A woman comments that in picking up the $1 bill they lost their $100 and ends with "There ya go. That's why boys are stupid." This is representative of our cultural understandings of men's cheating. We see cheating as something inherent to most men (if not all); we see cheating as simply men being "greedy"; and we regard men who cheat as stupid. Once we know a man previously cheated, we believe we know all that matters. We brand him a "cheater" and villainize him. So pervasive is this belief that often when people learn the topic of this book, they exclaim, "Pfft, I can you tell you why men cheat!" Self-proclaimed experts abound. They all reason no need for such a book or a study exists because they believe the reasons for men's cheating to be settled.

© The Author(s) 2020
A. M. Walker, *Chasing Masculinity*,
https://doi.org/10.1007/978-3-030-49818-4_1

The reality is that we likely know many men who participate in infidelity, men we like and admire and believe to be "good people." We just don't realize that they cheat. We may even look at their marriages from the outside with envy and admiration. These men are people we know, people whose company we enjoy. They are men who live next door, who work in the office two doors down, who take their kids to piano lessons, coach Little League, and open doors for their wives. The men we see doing all of those things are also the men who are logging on and hunting for a clandestine sexual partner to supplement their marriage. While we imagine affairs as something that happens between two people who played with fire by looking too long into one another's eyes, the men in this study made a conscious choice to seek out an outside partner online. And they did so after years of muddling through marital dynamics that left them feeling unsatisfied, unsupported, downtrodden, and like "less of a man." These men shared their unique perspectives and experiences, their feelings, their psyches, and their worlds. As much as you feel sure you know why men cheat, you likely don't have the first clue.

I conducted a yearlong investigation into extramarital experiences using a sample collected from *Ashley Madison*, a niche online dating site catering to married individuals seeking an outside partner. I collected rich interview data from 46 men between the ages of 27–70 located across the United States. Thirty-seven men (80%) in the study detailed dissatisfaction with the relational management in their primary partnerships. The men described emotionally unsatisfying primary partnerships, which lacked the level of praise, validation, and attention they desired. Most of the men mentioned having children. Thirty-five men (76% of the sample) reported sexless marriages. All of the men expressed discontent with the quality of their sexual lives within their marriages, specifically that they desired more sensuality in the encounters. Thirty-one men (67%) stated a need to remain in their primary partnership for the remainder of their lives. Among the other fifteen men, most expressed a desire to stay; only two men stated a plan to leave at some point in the future. All of the men in this inquiry created a profile on *Ashley Madison* to seek out an outside partner. Only three men were in the midst of their first affairs. The rest of the men reported involvement in subsequent affairs.

In their conversations with me about the affairs, these men spoke of a loss within their primary partnerships. These men spoke of a gradual slide over the years into feelings of emasculation, which they believed to be provoked by the state of their marriages. Men described sexual dynamics lacking sensuality and genuine enthusiasm on the part of their primary partners. They spoke of marriages where they no longer felt seen or valued. They believed their wives to be too "into themselves" and too wrapped up in their own lives to expend any energy investing in the men's concerns. They described their wives as disinterested in their feelings, their days, and what they had to offer as sexual partners. They reported that the loss of validation in their marriages made them feel like "less of a man." Eventually, they concluded that perhaps another woman might see them as interesting, worthy of praise and attention, and perhaps even sexually desirable. They set out to find such a woman by logging onto a website and creating a profile. For them, participation in infidelity presented an opportunity for validation, and affirmation of their sense of themselves as masculine, attractive, and wanted.

The men believed that their affairs helped them manage their emotional life and emotional responses to their primary partners toward whom they often felt resentment. Developing relationships with partners who expressed excitement to see them, demonstrated sexual desire for them, and sincerely asked about the events of their day, their feelings, and their dreams provided a much-needed boost to their sense of self-esteem and sense of themselves. Our cultural tendency is to imagine that women cheat for "attention" and men cheat for sex, but these men challenge those assumptions. In my previous book, *The Secret Life of the Cheating Wife*, the majority of women reported participation in affairs for sexual pleasure. They reported their motivation as sexual pleasure and orgasms, plain and simple. However, both books show that we should resist the temptation to gender infidelity. The majority of women in my previous book participated in outside partnerships in an effort to outsource the sexual aspect of their primary partnerships, however, they described rich emotional intimacy within those primary relationships. Thus, there existed no need to seek an emotional connection with a third party. For the seven women in that study who reported primary partnerships devoid of emotional support, emotional intimacy, and emotional connection, they also outsourced the emotional component of their primary partnerships. Thus, the difference in the participants' goals for participation in outside partnerships depended upon the state of their primary partnership not the gender of the participant.

Socially, the navigation of sexual relationships and monogamy is often perceived as private, but the reality is that "infidelity is a dynamic social process subject to influence by the context in which it is embedded" (Munsch 2015, p. 48). Looking at the practice of sexual non-consensual non-exclusivity among men involved in an assumed-monogamous primary partnership sheds light on intimate relationships as a whole. Examining what society frequently deems as deviant yields a better understanding of the average. Unpacking the dynamics of marriages where infidelity took place grants perspective on all marriages. Additionally, this study considers the experiences of men's participation in infidelity, a behavior often perceived as solely focused on men's sexual gratification. This sample of participants sought affairs to soothe the hurt feelings sustained in their marriages at the hands of spouses they believed to be disinterested in their lives, interests, and feelings. The purpose of this study was to investigate the experiences of meaning-making of men participating in outside partnerships, and to permit men to voice their lived experiences.

Importance of Marriage

The value of studying U.S. infidelity rests in the cultural importance of marriage in the United States. Though U.S. media representations present interest in marriage as specific to women, men highly value marriage as well. 2013 PEW Research Center data showed men report the desire to marry at the same rate women do (Cohn, 2013). Further, 2013 PEW data also revealed that men are more likely to remarry than women (64–52%). Cherlin explains, "Getting married is a way to show family and friends that you have a successful personal life. It is the ultimate merit badge" (Riccitelli, 2012, p. 205). Unsurprisingly, people list having a healthy marriage as one of their most important life goals (Karney, Garvan, & Thomas, 2003) and view having a stable, intimate relationship as essential to their happiness (Christopher & Sprecher, 2000).

The cultural attachment exists for good reason. Research shows that our romantic entanglements serve an important role in our well-being and health. Satisfying intimate relationships result in better physical health (Cohen et al., 1998), the ability to recover from illness more quickly (Kiecolt-Glaser et al., 2005), and a longer life (Gallo, Troxel, Matthews, & Kuller, 2003; Holt-Lundstad, Smith, & Layton, 2010). Studies show that healthy intimate relationships are the strongest predictor of happiness and emotional well-being (Diener & Seligman, 2002). In short, when in satisfying relationships, people function healthier both physically and mentally.

By contrast, when people live in distressed relationships or experience loneliness within their partnerships, their risk of both illness and depression increases (Cacioppo et al., 2002). Both loneliness and distressed relationships serve as chief reported reasons for seeking out therapy (Veroff, Kulka, & Douvan, 1981). The impact extends beyond the individual. Relationship distress and loneliness decrease worker productivity (Forthofer, Markman, Cox, Stanley, & Kessler, 1996). While the problem of loneliness may not grab headlines, recent research shows that experiencing loneliness puts individuals at risk for damaging behaviors. Loneliness proves as deadly as a nearly pack-a-day smoking habit; people reporting loneliness experience an increased risk of premature death as they are 50% more likely than those in healthy relationships (Tiwari, 2013). People benefit both in body and mind from functional and healthy marriages, and they suffer in unhealthy and dysfunctional ones.

The participants in this study reside in the United States, where monogamy is reified as "natural" throughout the culture. Most folks in this culture practice—or profess to—serial monogamy, where they go from one relationship to another but remain monogamous within those pairings for the life of the union. A single lifetime partner in a monogamous marriage functions as the ideal presented throughout U.S. culture. In the United States, 95% of Americans report a desire for a monogamous relationship (Treas & Giesen, 2000). Thus, in the United States the study of infidelity matters due to the high value placed on monogamous marriages.

Infidelity: The Ultimate Threat

Given the cultural value of marriage and monogamy in the United States, you likely register no surprise to learn that Americans report disapproval of infidelity for any reason (Wike, 2014). When the topic comes up at any social gathering, folks quickly disparage the practice. When marriages end and incidents of infidelity are revealed, people tend to blame the cheater for the relationship's demise. Regardless of how selfish, demanding, or difficult the other partner or how untenable the relationship's circumstances, people tend to lay the blame on the cheater. In the United States, the socially appropriate response to learning your partner cheated is ending the relationship. When we learn a spouse stayed after a known event of infidelity, we either pity them or regard them with disgust. Whatever bad behavior a partner displays, people will rationalize it by comparison to infidelity (e.g., "at least they're not cheating!"). When folks hear about cheating in someone else's relationship, they talk about the relief that their own relationship is monogamous. No one wants to discover they've been cheated on. No one wants to have to admit that they cheated in the past, or that they don't think cheating is a bad thing.

The data shows a gap between those who *want* monogamy and those who *practice* monogamy. How many people are cheating? Difficult to say for certain. Reports of the incidence of infidelity fluctuate greatly, often as a result of the method by which the data is collected. If I ask a participant "how many affairs have you ever had," the answer will be different than if I asked, "how many affairs have you had in the last year." If I ask a participant about their participation in infidelity in-person they're less likely to report honestly than if I asked over email, the internet, or even the phone. Additionally, people often "forget" to count sexual encounters where the memory is unpleasant, or where they failed to orgasm, or about which they feel guilty (Stombler & Baunach, 2010). Conceivably, that would omit a lot of instances of infidelity.

Further complicating the estimation of infidelity incidence? There exists no single definition of infidelity. In fact, two people in the same relationship may have completely different definitions regarding what "counts" as cheating and what doesn't because definitions are so individualized. Many couples promise monogamy but never define it, and instead assume that they both share the same definition. One partner may end up cheating according to the other partner's definition (unknown to the first partner), yet not according to their own. Partners may refrain from reporting instances that don't meet their own definition, but may cause (in their mind, unnecessary) conflict. Does oral sex count? It depends upon whom we ask. (Remember the Clinton scandal? Bill didn't count it.) Some folks think flirting is cheating. Others do not. For some, the disclosure of secrets counts. For others, it doesn't. Some count kissing. Others only sexual intercourse. All of this variance in terms of what "counts" muddles researchers' estimations of infidelity rates. Given the wide variation in definitions, many studies simply default to letting the participant count using their own definitions.

As a result of these blurred definitions, reliable and definitive rates of infidelity are both hard to come by and relatively new; existing rates often use measures that have been called into question (Atkins, Baucom, & Jacobson, 2001). For example, many of the existing calculations of infidelity rates are drawn from the General Social Survey (GSS) , which relies upon in-person interviews. Research shows that participants are less likely to admit to infidelity when asked as part of in-person interviews and surveys (Whisman & Snyder, 2007). Research using the GSS estimates the lifetime incidence of sexual infidelity to range between 20 and 37.5% (Atkins et al., 2001; Atkins & Kessel, 2008; Wiederman, 1997). Rates as high as 85.5% of married people committing infidelity have been reported (Yarob, Allgeier, & Sensibaugh, 1998). Researchers assume a general tendency to underestimate the incidence of infidelity (T. W. Smith, 1994). In short, we assume reported figures to be low. Even among dating couples, cheating occurs. Hertlein, Wetchler, and Piercy (2005) found that 30% of dating couples participate in some type of infidelity (Hertlein et al., 2005). As Hirsch et al. (2009) point out, infidelity is a "secret, but widespread (and widely acknowledged) social practice" (Hirsch et al., 2009, p. 3). The commonality between the data regarding incidence of infidelity is that at least some of us struggle with sexual exclusivity in marriages. The data shows at least some folks value monogamy more as a theory than a practice. The data illustrates that extramarital encounters are so common that affairs could be regarded as "an institutionalized part of the intimate and sexual landscape" (Kleese, 2011, p. 4).

Recent research shows an increasing incidence of cyber affairs. Tablets and smartphones grant more freedom to seek potential partners online. Stories of former lovers rekindling their relationship online through social media function as legend. Most of us know someone who knows someone who knows someone to whom this happened. James J. Sexton author of *If you're in my office, it's already too late*, claimed in a *Newsweek* interview that social media allows folks to connect with "people they don't have any business communicating with" which is "toxic" to marriages and makes "infidelity so easy now" (Wyne, 2018). Dating sites abound and membership isn't limited to bona fide singles. Married folks pose as single on *Match.com, Plenty of Fish*, etc. The increasing nature of this practice led to the creation of sites specifically for extra-relational sexual encounters—whether in consensually non-monogamous couplings or people participating in infidelity.

Commonsense discussions of infidelity place the cause of cheating either within the cheaters themselves, or due to a "real problem" in the relationship. People frequently posit that you wouldn't have cheated unless there was something wrong in the primary relationship. The widespread belief that "cheaters" are simply "bad people" or are people in "bad relationships" provides solace to many. That belief insulates many people from the threat of infidelity within their own relationship. After all, they assume their partner isn't a bad person, right? And they assume their own relationship isn't a bad relationship. True, there exists a correlation between relationship quality and infidelity. Satisfaction with the primary relationship and relationship quality, as well as sexual incompatibility and dissatisfaction, have all been cited as factors influencing participation in sexual non-exclusivity (Fisher et al., 2009; Mattingly, Wilson, Clark, Bequette, & Weidler, 2010; McAlister, Pachana, & Jackson, 2005; Preveti & Amato, 2004). Sexual incompatibility between spouses functions as an issue that significantly increases infidelity risk, especially disparities between levels of sexual desire (Regev, Zeiss, & Schmidt, 2006). For example, if a wife prefers daily sex, but her husband only gets in the mood for sex twice a month, then that couple must navigate a big disparity in desire levels. In such situations where dispari-ties between desire exist, the party with the higher level of sexual desire may wonder if anything will ever change, and feel doomed to keep going without if they stay in that relationship. At that point, their risk for participation in infidelity increases (Lewandowski & Ackerman, 2006). Some studies locate the cause of infidelity within the individual themselves (Dewall, Lambert, Slotter, Pond, Deckman, 2011; Mark, Milhausen, & Maitland, 2013; Treas & Giesen, 2000; Whisman & Snyder, 2007). However, data exists showing the causes of infidelity aren't quite so simple.

Studies show that even the presentation of an opportunity increases risk for participation in infidelity. That is, if someone finds themselves with an opportunity to cheat and they don't think they'll get caught, they're more likely to act on it (Dewall et al., 2011; Mark et al., 2013; Treas & Giesen, 2000; Whisman & Snyder, 2007). Evidence exists that infidelity with coworkers does not necessarily signal unhappiness in the primary relationship (Atkins et al., 2001; Treas & Giesen, 2000). In fact, some samples reported higher marital satisfaction than respon-dents involved with non-coworker outside partners (Wiggins & Lederer, 1984). These respondents reported the motivation for their affair was simply an opportunity to do so. This data suggests most of us capable of participation in infidelity, and points to the conclusion that infidelity fails to indicate a moral failing of the individual. While culturally we embrace monogamy as the ideal in the abstract, in our real lives, for many people just the presentation of an opportunity is all it takes to stray.

The discovery of infidelity in a relationship devastates. Infidelity renders people six times more likely to be diagnosed with a major depres-sive episode (Cano & O'Leary, 2000). Further, intimate partner violence and infidelity often exist together. Stories of people attacking, maiming, and even killing partners they *suspect* of infidelity remain prolific in the news. Infidelity ends many relationships when people simply cannot get over the betrayal of trust. However, the cheated-upon often carries that hurt into subsequent relationships. Some individuals struggle to trust anyone after discovery of a partner's infidelity.

Some people opt to rely on preventative measures, such as surveil-lance activities, e.g., monitoring their partner's emails, bank accounts, texts, or comings and goings. Social media abounds with memes and posts positing that granting your partner open access to your phone and accounts is a requirement of a "healthy" relationship, reasoning that if you're not cheating, there should be no problem. Men who perceive themselves to be at greater risk to be cheated on spend more time performing oral sex, and do so more often (Pham, Shackelford, & Sela, 2013). Conversely, women do not employ this strategy.

People often cite infidelity as a significant factor in both reports of marital distress and the decision to end marriages (Amato & Previti, 2003; Atkins, Yi, Baucom, & Christensen, 2005). Marital infidelity significantly increases the odds of divorce. It drives more couples to therapy, and therapists deem it the most difficult issue to resolve (Fife, Weeks, & Gambescia, 2008; Gordon, Baucom, & Snyder, 2005). In the United States, the commonsense thinking that "cheaters never change" makes repairing a relationship fractured by infidelity even more challenging. Generally speaking, our society remains unforgiving of those who cheat.

Fascination with Infidelity

Researchers devote much time, effort, and reporting to the topic of extramarital affairs. Infidelity results in broad consequences, making it an important social behavior. Although a key predictor of divorce and conflict within marriages, the causes of infidelity remain inadequately understood. Ultimately, the data fails to fully answer why some people participate in infidelity while others never do. While studies have tried, there exists no single archetype of a cheater.

Culturally, infidelity fascinates Americans—so long as the cheated *upon* isn't us. No one wants to discover that our partner is cheating. However, we gobble up with great interest stories of other couples' experiences with infidelity. Celebrity break-ups where infidelity is assumed or suspected serve as headlines. Media storms swirl around those in elected office found guilty by the court of public opinion. When couples dissolve without obvious provocation, we wonder if infidelity played a role.

While U.S. society generally holds privacy in high regard, when someone catches another person's partner cheating, they often feel obligated to report the behavior. A quick *Google* search will reveal stories of total strangers tattling on suspected cheaters observed in public spaces. When two women caught a glimpse of a woman's texts to her lover at a baseball game, they live-tweeted the unfolding drama. Many on social media claimed they deserved the Nobel Prize for informing the husband. Most people want privacy, but believe that cheaters don't deserve the same freedoms. The general consensus is if you cheat, you get what you deserve. The public discussions around the hacking of *Ashley Madison's* database reveal such a sentiment. In the face of the news of suicides and blackmailing, folks shrugged and cried, "That's what you get!" In fact, a 2018 study found that victims of the hacking also experienced victim-blaming because the focus rests on the moral implications of both the website itself and the intent of members, while ignoring the criminality of the breach (Cross, Parker, & Sansom, 2018). People openly scorned and mocked *Ashley Madison* users (Hackathorn, Daniels, Ashdown, Rife, & Rife, 2017). Media interest in the event proved prolific. Lots of companies experienced large-scale data breaches in recent history (e.g., Hilton, *LinkedIn*, Target, J. P. Morgan, Home Depot, Sony, etc.), but another researcher found that the *Ashley Madison* hack generated the greatest number of column inches in the press (Mansfield-Devine, 2015). In the United States, infidelity proves both newsworthy and gossip-worthy, as well as fodder for self-righteous attitudes.

Sexual Satisfaction and Relationship Quality

How important is sexual satisfaction in a long-term relationship? If you believe the data, pretty important. Researchers use the term sexual satisfaction to refer to the level at which people report being satisfied with the ways their relationship meets their sexual needs. Sexual satisfaction serves as an indicator of sexual health, and correlates strongly with overall relationship satisfaction (Pascoal, Narciso, & Pereira, 2014). Long-term sexual satisfaction is negatively correlated with conflict within the partnership (Hanning et al., 2007). In other words, if a couple is having good sex often enough, the other problems in the relationship tend to seem less important. Sex functions as the figurative glue binding couples together, and the lubricant to help them glide through frustrations.

Culturally, the assumption persists that if a couple "loves" one another, good sex will certainly follow. In reality, couples commonly report sexual incompatibility as a marital issue. Only 48% of men and 58% of women report satisfaction with the current frequency of sex in their marriages (A. Smith et al., 2011). Loving someone and having the capacity to share a home and a life together do not automatically predict sexual compatibility. Why does this matter? Within couples, individuals reporting dissatisfaction with sexual frequency are also more likely to report dissatisfaction with the overall relational aspects of their relationships (McNulty, Wenner, & Fisher, 2016; A. Smith et al., 2011). Dissatisfaction with the sexual elements of a relationship breeds dissatisfaction with the relationship as a whole. Therefore, we need to get interested in the ways unsatisfying sex impacts marriage and how to resolve that, as well as the ways what happens *before* couples breach the bedroom door comes to bear on sexual satisfaction.

The Burden of Masculinity

We conceive of gender as something we "are," something inherent to us from birth. But the reality is that we perform gender daily as an expression of what current social norms deem as "natural" and this performance is messy, dynamic, and must be enacted in routine everyday interactions and practices (Goffman, 1987; West & Zimmerman, 1987). These performances of gender and the results of those acts have social implications for both the actor themselves and society as a whole.

The term "masculinity" is often used in popular discourse, and serves as the description for the social expectations of men in any given society. Within research on masculinity, the concept of hegemonic masculinity proves important. Hegemonic masculinity relies upon current social norms around gendered behavior and serves as the most sought-after and popular conception of masculinity in a specific social context (Carrigan, Connell, & Lee, 1985; Connell, 1987; Connell & Messerschmidt,

2005; Epstein, 2006; Frank, Kehler, Lovell, & Davidson, 2003). Popular discourse often refers to this as the "alpha male" or "ideal man." In essence, hegemonic masculinity answers the question, "What does it mean to be a man right now?" As R. W. Connell posits, "hegemonic masculinity is highly visible" (Connell & Messerschmidt, 2005, p. 209), and acts as the privileged form of masculinity, which informs and shapes how men define manhood for themselves and how society determines what forms of manhood exist as less acceptable.

In reality, few men can actually perform the hegemonic masculinity in their culture, but men still endorse it as ideal. These performances of masculinity—both hegemonic and non-hegemonic—often serve as an attempt in self-protection against the stigma of both ridicule for failure to "live up" to the demands of masculinity and the experience of emasculation. Jefferson explains "boys and men choose these discursive positions that help them ward off anxiety and avoid feelings of powerlessness" (Connell & Messerschmidt, 2005, p. 842). Many men feel pressure to demonstrate manliness to some degree.

The performance of masculinity is continual and constant. No moment exists where society pronounces a man as "masculine enough." No event occurs where someone rates his masculinity high enough to render him exempt from its constant and conscious performance. Thus, men's performance of masculinity results in pronounced stress and anxiety as it functions as an attempt to prove their manliness in the form of a formalized ritual (Gilmore, 1990; Kimmel, 2006). Further, even the successful performance of masculinity can negatively impact a man's relationships and sense of self (Levant & Richmond, 2007). For example, a man's refusal to perform child-rearing activities—as these are not deemed traditionally masculine behaviors—may result in their partner's decreased satisfaction in the relationship.

Further, researchers theorize that because current conceptions of manhood in U.S. society devalue emotional expression, attempts to accomplish idealized forms of manhood in a society render a man unable to process, feel, or express emotions (Levant & Richmond, 2007). An inability to process, identify, and express emotions creates additional obstacles in the formation and maintenance of intimate personal relationships. Additionally, due to the stigma attached to seeking help for mental health in terms of masculinity, men tend to avoid addressing mental health issues (Jakupcak, Blais, Grossbard, Garcia, & Okiishi, 2014; Vogel, Wester, Hammer, & Downing-Matibag, 2014). This also impacts men's relationships, as well as their own well-being. Research shows that conformity to traditional masculine practices and behaviors can negatively impact relationship satisfaction for both men and women within heterosexual pairings (Burn & Ward, 2005; Coughlin & Wade, 2012).

Aside from the ramifications on romantic relationships and mental health, the performance of masculinity also impacts physical health (Blazina & Watkins, 1996; Caswell, Bosson, Vandello, & Sellers, 2014; Eisler & Skidmore, 1987; Robertson, 2007). Research also shows a clear link between men perceiving a challenge to their masculinity and criminal behavior, domestic violence, and even murder-suicides (Anderson & Umberson, 2001; Krienert, 2003; Oliffe, Ogrodniczuk, Bottorff, Johnson, & Hoyak, 2012). Men who embrace forms of masculinity that value risk-taking, toughness, and self-sufficiency have higher rates of accidents and other preventable health risks (Courtenay, 2000).

Because men must consistently prove themselves as manly, they need to engage in displays of manliness. A team of researchers found that when men were asked to perform tasks traditionally regarded as feminine, for example, braiding their daughter's hair, these actions served as gender-threatening, and men elected to subsequently engage in aggressive displays of manliness, namely, violence (Bosson, Vandello, Burnaford, Weaver, & Wasti, 2009). When they perceive their manliness being threatened in some way, many men tend to engage in aggressive gender-reinforcing behavior in an effort to restore their manliness. Research shows that men differ considerably from women in how they respond to perceived gender threats. A 2014 study found men perceive the loss of employment as a threat to gender identity (Michniewicz, Vandello, & Bosson, 2014). Thus, along with the financial strain to his family, his loved ones must also contend with his response to threatened masculinity.

Research demonstrates the reality that a man's sense of himself as masculine is bestowed by the public, not by the man himself

(Weaver, Vandello, Bosson, & Burnaford, 2010). Ultimately, attainment of society's "ideal manhood" is hard—if not impossible—to accomplish, requires continuous proof in social settings, and is primarily granted to a man by others (Vandello, Bosson, Cohen, Burnaford, & Weaver, 2008; Vandello & Bosson, 2013). Thus, masculinity functions as a desired identity, but proves unattainable. Even when briefly won, it's inevitably lost through its performance, and most of its performance is for the benefit of other men (Kimmel, 1994). This leads to ongoing anxiety for men who desire to perform masculinity (Vandello & Bosson, 2013; Vandello et al., 2008). Thus, the expectations of masculinity often function as a burden in a man's life.

Gendered Sexuality and Infidelity

Despite advances in attitudes toward gender, cheating remains the perceived domain of men. The response to the news of men's infidelity often includes shrugs and a comment akin to "boys will be boys." U.S. attitudes position men as sexual aggressors with insatiable appetites, who would thusly cheat to sate those desires. In fact, men's masculinity is in part built upon sexual prowess (Fine, Weis, Addelston, & Marusza, 1997; Flood, Gardiner, Pease, & Pringle, 2007; Halkitis, Green, & Wilton, 2004; Kimmel, Hearn, & Connell, 2005; Thorne, 1993). For a man to maintain his masculinity, he needs to amass a list of past sexual partners, and frequently demonstrate both his insatiable sexual desire, and his sexual expertise (Fields et al., 2015; Flood et al., 2007; Halkitis et al., 2004; Pascoe, 2011; Ramírez, 1999). Further, he is to be assertive, independent, and dominant, including within sexual situations (Kiefer & Sanchez, 2007). Men who adhere to expectations of traditional masculinity may tend toward competitiveness, which the men in this study reported with regard to besting other men sexually, and restricted emotional expression, which the men in this study reported as well (Sanchez & Crocker, 2005).

The double standard requires women to at least feign limited sexual experience, or face slut-shaming. By contrast, men are regarded as "studs" when they engage in frequent sexual couplings with a variety of partners.

The commonsense understanding of sexuality is that men want to have a lot of sex—and have it with a lot of different partners—and women do not. However, many researchers posit that findings supporting that idea are likely due to socialization that teaches that women aren't *supposed* to desire sex. Socialization teaches women that they must feel love for a partner to want sex, while teaching men to desire recreational sex. This socialization often impacts self-reporting of both sexual behavior and sexual motivations (Alexander & Fisher, 2003; Conley, 2011; Eastwick & Finkel, 2008; Milhausen & Herold, 2000).

Additionally, the socialization that teaches men to be self-focused, and thus more attentive to own their needs, also teaches women to both sublimate and ignore their own needs to instead focus on the needs of others. Many men go into long-term relationships feeling the pressure to provide both financially and sexually, and without the tools to function as an equal emotional partner. Men often look to women to perform relational management to manage the emotional life of the relationship as well as their own emotional needs (More on this in Chapter 3). Meanwhile, they rely on their partner's orgasm to reify their masculinity (More on this in Chapter 8). That's a lot of pressure on a marriage and a lot of responsibility placed on one single person in your life.

Current U.S. conceptions of masculinity paint "real men" as sexually aggressive and driven by intense and unrelenting sexual desire. While the assumption is that women prefer monogamy, we paint men as craving sexual variety. The findings of my previous study challenge those assumptions. The majority of those women reported seeking sexual encounters solely for sexual pleasure, and vetting partners to avoid emotional entanglements (Walker, 2018). (Again, those women also reported primary partnerships with rich emotional intimacy.) Further, research reveals that relationship and sexual dynamics function with far greater nuance than common discourse acknowledges. For husbands, the greater their wives' sexual satisfaction, the greater the husbands' relationship satisfaction (Yoo, Bartle-Haring, Day, & Gangamma, 2014). Thus, their partner's enthusiasm, enjoyment, and pleasure factor heavily into their own satisfaction with the pairing. Women often fake orgasms rather than risk the hit to their male partner's self-esteem because men's masculinity rests on sexual prowess as demonstrated through their partner's orgasm (More on this in Chapter 8). Her orgasm functions as evidence of masculinity, which in turn provokes his experience of pleasure.

Theoretical Perspective

This work is complicated by the existing frameworks of masculinity, which often fail to consider the role of men's sexual lives and sexual selves. At present, "limited research exists concerning the relationship between masculinity and sexual satisfaction" (Daniel, 2013, p. 345). The findings in this study certainly suggest that men's sense of themselves as a sexual actor impacts their sense of themselves as a masculine person. "It is becoming more clear that the role of masculinity is a key factor in the mental and physical health of men, especially as they form their own sense of selves both sexually and otherwise" (Daniel, 2013, p. 345). Thus, this work offers a glimpse into men's perceptions and rationales for their sexual lives and their sense of their own masculinity.

The Infidelity Workaround

In my first book, I reported that women exercised participation in infidelity as a workaround. Specifically, for those women, outside partnerships functioned as a workaround to avoid the pain, inconvenience, financial ramifications, and stigma of divorce. Most of the women in that study reported seeking outside partnerships in an effort to outsource the sexual aspect of their marriages in a search for sexual pleasure in the form of orgasms, while reporting primary partnerships replete with emotional intimacy. With those needs met, the women lacked a need to search for emotional connection.

The men in this book also employ the Infidelity Workaround. They participate in outside partnerships as a workaround to avoid the pain, financial ramifications, stigma, and inconvenience of a divorce. However, they seek outside partnerships in an effort to outsource the emotional aspect of their marriages. Their search focuses on unmet emotional needs rather than chasing orgasms. Like the seven women in the previous study whose primary partners failed to meet their emotional needs, these men outsourced the emotional component of their primary partnerships to sexual outside partnerships.

Overview of Men's Infidelity Workaround

The men in this study reported a belief that their primary partners lacked interest in them and were "impossible to please." As a result of those perceptions, men believed themselves a constant disappointment to their primary partners. The dynamics of the marital bed added to their sense of failure. The men in this study made clear that they needed regular praise and that they relied upon their female partner to provide what I call "relational management," a term which refers to the actions of female partners to help men manage their own emotional life (e.g., asking about his feelings). Men stated clearly that they needed a female partner to pay a lot of attention to them, provide frequent praise, show interest in the mundane details of their days, and provide relational management. This failure to hold their partner's interest stood as a threat to their sense of themselves as masculine, and a source of a great deal of hurt and upset at their unmet emotional needs. They turned to outside partnerships as a workaround: an attempt to get their needs met without enduring the pain of upending their lives via divorce. Like the women in my previous study, they sought to remain in their primary partnerships for a host of reasons, including the tremendous affection they held for their primary partners. But they also believed themselves incapable of continuing to go on without getting their needs met. Thus, the Infidelity Workaround served to meet unmet needs without creating new hurts and struggles that would surely accompany a divorce.

As a result of men's belief that they no longer held their primary partners' interest, they sought outside partners who would both show interest in them and provide sensual sexual encounters, which served as validation of their sexual prowess, which in turn validates their sense of themselves as masculine. Men spoke of the importance of feeling desired and wanted, but also the need for an emotional connection (i.e., showing caring, interest in their day, and provision of relational management) with their outside partner. These men spoke of feeling pressure to perform sexually, so as to continue seeing their outside partners. Men feared being laughed at or made fun of as a result of a poor sexual performance. Most importantly, for the men in this study, their partner's orgasm served as validation of them as sexually skilled, and thus masculine. Because sexual performance exists as bound up in masculinity, for these men, the provision of women's orgasms functions as their responsibility. They perceive their ability to provoke orgasm as a special skill. Men believed their outside partnerships to provide healing, making it possible to remain in their primary partnerships and to function as a better partner. For them, the Infidelity Workaround functioned to keep their marriages together while outsourcing their unmet emotional needs to a more interested third party.

Conclusion

This book focuses on the meaning-making and experiences of men in the United States who purposefully sought out extramarital relationships online. These men did not fall into an affair due to opportunity. They created their own opportunities by logging on, creating a profile, and vetting potential partners. For these men, ending their marriages was not an attractive option, and living with unmet emotional needs proved untenable. To avoid the hurt, financial challenges, stigma, and upset of a divorce, the men engaged in the Infidelity Workaround, in an effort to outsource the emotional aspect of their primary partnerships to a more enthusiastic third party.

This book gives voice to their experiences and perceptions through participation in in-depth interviews regarding the role of outside partnerships in their lives and the impact upon their marriages. The participants were all members of *Ashley Madison*, a site devoted to helping married people seeking outside partners. Examining these men's experiences is important as it provides a glimpse into the interworking of our most intimate relationships and considers the ways men navigate marriages that fall short of their expectations. Further, the ways their experiences prove both similar to and different from the women of my previous book, who also sought outside partners on *Ashely Madison*, provides valuable insight into marital dynamics and our commonsense narratives about gender.

Outside partnerships functioned to boost the men's perception of their masculinity in an effort to address the emasculation they felt within their primary partnerships. But more importantly, these outside partners provided highly valued emotional support and validation (i.e., relational management), as well as non-rushed, sensual sexual encounters, which made men feel virile and sexually skilled, but more importantly, desired and wanted. Men spoke at length about the value of sexual events featuring sensuality, where the acts weren't rushed with a partner who brought enthusiasm and passion to the bedroom as well as demonstrating sexual desire for them as a lover. However, the emotional support, validation and praise, and the provision of relational management proved of the highest value to the men in this study.

References

Alexander, M. G., & Fisher, T. D. (2003). Truth and consequences: Using the bogus pipeline to examine differences in self-reported sexuality. *The Journal of Sex Research, 40*(1), 27–35. https://doi.org/10.1080/002244903 09552164.

Amato, P. R., & Previti, D. (2003). People's reasons for divorcing: Gender, social class, the life course, and adjustment. *Journal of Family Issues, 24*(5), 602–626. https://doi.org/10.1177/0192513x03024005002.

Anderson, K. L., & Umberson, D. (2001). Gendering violence: Masculinity and power in men's accounts of domestic violence. *Gender and Society, 15*(3), 358–380. https://doi.org/10.1177/089124301015003003.

Atkins, D. C., & Kessel, D. E. (2008). Religiousness and infidelity: Attendance, but not faith and prayer, predict marital infidelity. *Journal of Marriage and Family, 70*, 407–418. https://doi.org/10.1111/j.1741-3737.2008.00490.x.

Atkins, D. C., Baucom, D. H., & Jacobson, N. S. (2001). Understanding infidelity: Correlates in a national random sample. *Journal of Family Psychology, 15*, 735–749. https://doi.org/10.1037/0893-3200.15.4.735.

Atkins, D. C., Yi, J., Baucom, D. H., & Christensen, A. (2005). Infidelity in couples seeking marital therapy. *Journal of Family Psychology, 19*, 470–473. https://doi.org/10.1037/0893-3200.19.3.470.

Blazina, C., & Watkins, C. E., Jr. (1996). Masculine gender role conflict: Effects on college men's psychological well-being, chemical substance usage, and attitudes towards help-seeking. *Journal of Counseling Psychology, 43*(4), 461–465. https://doi.org/10.1037/0022-0167.43.4.461.

Bosson, J. K., Vandello, J. A., Burnaford, R. M., Weaver, J. R., & Wasti, S. A. (2009). Precarious manhood and displays of physical aggression. *Personality and Social Psychology Bulletin, 35*(5), 623–634. https://doi.org/10.1177/014 6167208331161.

Burn, S. M., & Ward, A. Z. (2005). Men's conformity to traditional masculinity and relationship satisfaction. *Psychology of Men & Masculinity, 6*(4), 254–263. https://doi.org/10.1037/1524-9220.6.4.254.

Cacioppo, J. T., Hawkley, L. C., Crawford, L. E., Ernst, J. M., Burleson, M. H., Kowalweski, R. B., … Bernston, G. G. (2002). Loneliness and health: Potential mechanisms. *Psychosomatic Medicine, 64*, 407–417. https://doi.org/10.1097/00006842-200205000-00005.

Cano, A., & O'Leary, K. D. (2000). Infidelity and separations precipitate major depressive episodes and symptoms of nonspecific depression and anxiety. *Journal of Consulting and Clinical Psychology, 68*, 774–781. https://doi.org/10.1037/0022-006x.68.5.774.

Carrigan, T., Connell, B., & Lee, J. (1985). Toward a new sociology of masculinity. *Theory and Society, 14*(5), 551–604.

Caswell, T. A., Bosson, J. K., Vandello, J. A., & Sellers, J. G. (2014). Testosterone and men's stress responses to gender threats. *Psychology of Men & Masculinity, 15*(1), 4–11.

Christopher, F. S., & Sprecher, S. (2000). Sexuality in marriage, dating, and other relationships: A decade in review. *Journal of Marriage and the Family, 62*(4), 999–1017. https://doi.org/10.1111/j.1741-3737.2000.00999.x.

Cohen, S., Frank, E., Doyle, W. J., Skoner, D. P., Rabin, B. S., Jack M., & Gwaltney, J. (1998). Types of stressors that increase susceptibility to the common cold in healthy adults. *Health Psychology,17*, 214–223. https://doi.org/10.1037/0278-6133.17.3.214.

Cohn, D. V. (2013). Love and marriage. *Pew Research Center.* Retrieved from https://www.pewsocialtrends.org/2013/02/13/love-and-marriage/.

Conley, T. D. (2011). Perceived proposer personality characteristics and gender differences in acceptance of casual sex offers. *Journal of Personality and Social Psychology, 100*, 309–329. https://doi.org/10.1037/a0022152.

Connell, R. W. (1987). *Gender and power.* Sydney, AU: Allen and Urwi.

Connell, R. W., & Messerschmidt, J. W. (2005). Hegemonic masculinity: Rethinking the concept. *Gender and Society, 19*(6), 829–859. https://doi.org/10.1177/0891243205278639.

Coughlin, P., & Wade, J. C. (2012). Masculinity ideology, income disparity, and romantic relationship quality among men with higher earning female partners. *Sex Roles, 67*(5–6), 311–322. https://doi.org/10.1007/s11199-012-0187-6.

Courtenay, W. H. (2000). Constructions of masculinity and their influence on men's wellbeing: A theory of gender and health. *Social Science and Medicine, 50*(10), 1385–1401.

Cross, C., Parker, M., & Sansom, D. (2018). Media discourses surrounding 'non-ideal' victims: The case of the Ashley Madison data breach. *International Review of Victimology, 25*(4). https://doi.org/10.1177/026975801775 2410.

Daniel, S. (2013). The relationships among body image, masculinity, and sexual satisfaction in men. *Psychology of Men & Masculinities, 14*(4), 345–351.

Dewall, C. N., Lambert, N. M., Slotter, E. B., Pond, R. S., Jr., & Deckman, T. (2011). So far away from one's partner, Yet so close to alternatives: Avoidant attachment, interest in alternatives, and infidelity. *Journal of Personality and Social Psychology, 101*(6), 1302–1316. https://doi.org/10.1037/a0025497.

Diener, E., & Seligman, M. E. P. (2002). Very happy people. *Psychological Science, 13,* 81–84. https://doi.org/10.1111/1467-9280.00415.

Eastwick, P. W., & Finkel, E. J. (2008). Sex differences in mate preference revisited: Do people know what they initially desire in a romantic partner. *Journal of Personality and Social Psychology, 94*(2), 245–264. https://doi.org/10.1037/0022-3514.94.2.245.

Eisler, R. M., & Skidmore, J. R. (1987). Masculine gender role stress: Scale development and component factors in the appraisal of stressful situations. *Behavior Modification, 11*(2), 123–136. https://doi.org/10.1177/014544558 70112001.

Epstein, D. (2006). Real boys don't work: 'Underachievement', masculinity, and the harassment of 'sissies'. In D. Epstein, J. Elwood, V. Hey, & J. Maw (Eds.), *Failing boys: Issues in gender and achievement* (pp. 96–108). Buckingham, UK: Open University Press.

Fields, E. L., Bogart, L. M., Smith, K. C., Malebranche, D. J., Ellen, J., & Schuster, M. A. (2015). "I always felt I had to prove my manhood": Homosexuality, masculinity, gender role strain, and HIV risk among young black men who have sex with men. *American Journal of Public Health, 105*(1), 122–131. https://doi.org/10.2105/AJPH.2013.301866.

Fife, S. T., Weeks, G. R., & Gambescia, N. (2008). Treating infidelity: An integrative approach. *The Family Journal: Counseling and Therapy for Couples and Families, 16,* 316–323. https://doi.org/10.1177/1066480708323205.

Fine, M., Weis, L., Addelston, J., & Marusza, J. (1997). (In)secure times: Constructing white working-class masculinities in the late 20th century. *Gender & Society, 11*(1), 52–68. https://doi.org/10.1177/089124397011 001004.

Fisher, A. D., Corona, G., Bandini, E., Mannucci, E., Lotti, F., Boddi, V., … Maggi, M. (2009). Psychobiological correlates of extramarital affairs and differences between stable and occasional infidelity among men with sexual dysfunctions. *The Journal of Sexual Medicine, 6*(3), 866–875. https://doi.org/10.1111/j.1743-6109.2008.01140.x.

Flood, M., Gardiner, J. K., Pease, B., & Pringle, K. (2007). *International encyclopedia of men and masculinities.* Abington, OX: Routledge.

Forthofer, M. S., Markman, H. J., Cox, M., Stanley, S., & Kessler, R. C. (1996). Associations between marital distress and work loss in a national sample. *Journal of Marriage and the Family, 58,* 597–605. https://doi.org/10.2307/353720.

Frank, B., Kehler, M., Lovell, T., & Davidson, K. (2003). A tangle of trouble: Boys, masculinity, and schooling-future directions. *Educational Review, 55*(2), 119–133. https://doi.org/10.1080/00131910303262.

Gallo, L. C., Troxel, W. M., Matthews, K. A., & Kuller, L. H. (2003). Marital status and quality in middle-aged women: Associations with levels and trajectories of cardiovascular risk factors. *Health Psychology, 22,* 453–463. https://doi.org/10.1037/0278-6133.22.5.453.

Gilmore, D. D. (1990). *Manhood in the making: Cultural concepts of masculinity* New Haven. Conn: Yale University Press.

Goffman, E. (1987). The arrangement between the sexes. *Theory and Society, 4*(3), 301–333.

Gordon, K. C., Baucom, D. H., & Snyder, D. K. (2005). Treating couples recovering from infidelity: An integrative approach. *Journal of Clinical Psychology, 61,* 1393–1405. https://doi.org/10.1002/jclp.20189.

Hackathorn, J., Daniels, J., Ashdown, B. K., Rife, S. C., & Rife, S. C. (2017). From fear and guilt: Negative perceptions of Ashley Madison users. *Psychology & Sexuality, 8*(1–2), 41–54. https://doi.org/10.1080/19419899.2017.1316767.

Halkitis, P. N., Green, K. A., & Wilton, L. (2004). Masculinity, body image, and sexual behavior in HIV-seropositive gay men: A two-phase formative behavioral investigation using the internet. *International Journal of Men's Health, 3*(1), 27–42.

Hanning, R. V., O'Keefe, S. L., Randall, E. J., Kommor, M. J., Baker, E., & Wilson, R. (2007). Intimacy orgasm likelihood and conflict predict sexual satisfaction in heterosexual male and female respondents. *Journal of Sex & Marital Therapy, 33*(22), 93–113. https://doi.org/10.1080/00926230601098449.

Hertlein, K. M., Wetchler, J. L., & Piercy, F. P. (2005). Infidelity. *Journal of couple & relationship therapy: Innovations in clinical and educational interventions, 4*(2–3), 5–16. https://doi.org/10.1300/J398v04n02_02.

Hirsch, J. S., Wardlow, H., Smith, D. J., Phinney, H. M., Parikh, S., & Nathanson, C. A. (2009). *The secret: Love, marriage and HIV*. Nashville, TN: Vanderbilt University.

Holt-Lundstad, J., Smith, T. B., & Layton, J. B. (2010). Social relationships and mortality risk: A meta-analytic review. *PLoS Medicine, 7*(7), e100316. https://doi.org/10.1371/journal.pmed.1000316.

Jakupcak, M., Blais, R. K., Grossbard, J., Garcia, H., & Okiishi, J. (2014). "Toughness" in association with mental health symptoms among Iraq and Afghanistan war veterans seeking veterans affairs health care. *Psychology of Men & Masculinity, 15*(1), 100–104. https://doi.org/10.1037/a0031508.

Karney, B. R., Garvan, C. W., & Thomas, M. S. (2003). *Family formation in Florida: 2003 Baseline survey of attitudes, beliefs, and demographics relating to marriage and family formation*. Gainesville, FL: University of Florida, Department of Psychology.

Kiecolt-Glaser, J. K., Loving, T. J., Stowell, J. R., Malarkey, W. B., Lemeshow, S., Dickinson, S. L., & Glaser, R. (2005). Hostile marital interactions, proinflammatory cytokine production, and wound healing. *Archives of General Psychiatry, 62*, 1377–1384. https://doi.org/10.1001/archpsyc.62.12.1377.

Kiefer, A. K., & Sanchez, D. T. (2007). Scripting sexual passivity: A gender role perspective. *Personal Relationships, 14*, 269–290. https://doi.org/10.1111/j.1475-6811.2007.00154.x.

Kimmel, M. S. (1994). Masculinity as homophobia: Fear, shame, and silence in the construction of gender identity. In H. W. Brod & M. Kaufman (Eds.), *Theorizing masculinities* (pp. 119–141). London: Sage.

Kimmel, M. S. (2006). *Manhood in America: A cultural history*. New York: Oxford University Press.

Kimmel, M. S., Hearn, J., & Connell, R. W. (2005). *Handbook of studies on men and masculinities*. Thousand Oaks, CA: Sage.

Kleese, C. (2011). Notions of love in polyamory: Elements in a discourse on multiple loving. *Labratorium, 3*(2), 4–25.

Krienert, J. L. (2003). Masculinity and crime: A quantitative exploration of Messerschmidt's hypothesis. *Electronic Journal of Sociology, 7*(2), 1–30.

Levant, R. F., & Richmond, K. (2007). A review of research on masculinity ideologies using the male role norms inventory. *The Journal of Men's Studies, 15*(2), 130–146. https://doi.org/10.3149/jms.1502.130.

Lewandowski, G. W., & Ackerman, R. A. (2006). Something's missing: Need fulfillment and self-expansion as predictors of susceptibility to infidelity. *Journal of Social Psychology, 146*(4), 389–403. https://doi.org/10.3200/socp. 146.4.389-403.

Mansfield-Devine, S. (2015). The ashley madison affair. *Network Security, 9,* 8–16. https://doi.org/10.1016/S1353-4858(15)30080-5.

Mark, K. P., Milhausen, R. R., & Maitland, S. B. (2013). The impact of sexual compatibility on sexual and relationship satisfaction in a sample of young adult heterosexual couples. *Sexual and Relationship Therapy, 28*(3), 201–214. https://doi.org/10.1080/14681994.2013.807336.

Mattingly, B. A., Wilson, K., Clark, E. M., Bequette, A. W., & Weidler, D. J. (2010). Foggy faithfulness: Relationship quality, religiosity, and the perceptions of dating infidelity scale in an adult sample. *Journal of Family Issues, 31*(11), 1465–1480. https://doi.org/10.1177/0192513x10362348.

McAlister, A., Pachana, N., & Jackson, C. J. (2005). Predictors of young dating adults' inclination to engage in extradyadic sexual activities: A multi-perspective study. *British Journal of Psychology, 96,* 331–350. https://doi.org/ 10.1348/000712605x47936.

McNulty, J. K., Wenner, C. A., & Fisher, T. D. (2016). Longitudinal associations among relationship satisfaction, sexual satisfaction, and frequency of sex in early marriage. *Archives of Sexual Behavior, 45*(1), 85–97. https://doi. org/10.1007/s10508-014-0444-6.

Michniewicz, K. S., Vandello, J. A., & Bosson, J. K. (2014). Men's (mis) perceptions of the gender threatening consequences of unemployment. *Sex Roles, 7*(3–4), 88–97. https://doi.org/10.1007/s11199-013-0339-3.

Milhausen, R. R., & Herold, E. S. (2000). Does the sexual double standard still exist? Perceptions of university women. *The Journal of Sex Research, 36*(4), 361–368. https://doi.org/10.1080/00224499909552008.

Munsch, C. L. (2015). Her support, his support: Money, masculinity, and marital infidelity. *American Sociological Review, 80*(3), 469–495. https://doi. org/10.1177/0003122415579989.

Oliffe, J. L., Ogrodniczuk, J. S., Bottorff, J. L., Johnson, J. L., & Hoyak, K. A. K. (2012). "You feel like you can't live anymore": Suicide from the perspectives of Canadian men who experience depression. *Social Science and Medicine, 74*(4), 506–514. https://doi.org/10.1016/j.socscimed.2010. 03.057.

Pascoal, P. M., Narciso, I. d. S. B., & Pereira, N. M. (2014). What is sexual satisfaction? Thematic analysis of lay people's definitions. *Journal of Sex Research, 51*(1), 22–30. https://doi.org/10.1080/00224499.2013.815149.

Pascoe, C. J. (2011). *Dude, you're a fag masculinity and sexuality in high school, with a new preface.* Berkeley and Los Angeles: University of California Press.

Pham, M. N., Shackelford, T., & Sela, Y. (2013). Women's oral sex behaviors and risk of partner infidelity. *Personality and Individual Differences, 55*(4), 446–449. https://doi.org/10.1016/j.paid.2013.04.008.

Preveti, D., & Amato, P. R. (2004). Is infidelity a cause or consequence of poor marital quality? *Journal of Social and Personal Relationships, 21,* 217–230. https://doi.org/10.1177/0265407504041384.

Ramírez, R. L. (1999). *What it means to be a man: Reflections on Puerto Rican masculinity.* New Brunswick, NJ: Rutgers.

Regev, L. G., Zeiss, A., & Schmidt, J. P. (2006). Low sexual desire. In J. E. Fisher & W. T. O'Donohue (Eds.), *Practitioner's guide to evidence psychotherapy* (pp. 377–385). New York: Springer.

Riccitelli, J. M. (2012). *You may now kiss the bride: Biblical principles for lifelong marital happiness.* Bloomington, IN: Westbow.

Robertson, S. (2007). *Understanding men and health: Masculinities, identity and wellbeing.* UK: McGraw-Hill Education.

Sanchez, D. T., & Crocker, J. (2005). Why investment in gender ideals affects well-being: The role of external contingencies of self-worth. *Psychology of Women Quarterly, 29*(1), 63–77. https://doi.org/10.1111/j.1471-6402.2005.00169.x.

Smith, T. W. (1994). Attitudes toward sexual permissiveness: Trends, correlates, and behavioral connections. In A. S. Rossi (Ed.), *Sexuality across the life course* (pp. 63–97). Chicago: University of Chicago Press.

Smith, A., Lyons, A., Ferris, J., Richters, J., Pitts, M., Shelley, J., & Simpson, J. M. (2011). Sexual and relationship satisfaction among heterosexual men and women: The importance of desired frequency of sex. *Journal of Sex & Marital Therapy, 37*(2), 104–115. https://doi.org/10.1080/0092623X.2011.560531.

Stombler, M., & Baunach, D. M. (2010). *Doing it differently: Men's and women's estimates of their number of lifetime sexual partners.* Boston, MA: Allyn and Bacon.

Thorne, B. (1993). *Gender play: Girls and boys in school.* New Brunswick, NJ: Rutgers University Press.

Tiwari, S. C. (2013). Loneliness: A disease? *Indian Journal of Psychiatry, 55*(4), 320–322. https://doi.org/10.4103/0019-5545.120536.

Treas, J., & Giesen, D. (2000). Sexual infidelity among married and cohabiting Americans. *Journal of Marriage and the Family, 62*(1), 48–60. https://doi.org/10.1111/j.1741-3737.2000.00048.x.

Vandello, J. A., & Bosson, J. K. (2013). Hard won and easily lost: A review and synthesis of theory and research on precarious manhood. *Psychology of Men & Masculinity, 14*(2), 101–113. https://doi.org/10.1037/a0029826.

Vandello, J. A., Bosson, J., Cohen, D., Burnaford, R. M., & Weaver, J. R. (2008). Precarious manhood. *Journal of Personality and Social Psychology, 95*(6), 1325–1339. https://doi.org/10.1037/a0012453.

Veroff, J., Kulka, R. A., & Douvan, E. A. M. (1981). *Mental health in America: Patterns of helpseeking from 1957 to 1976*. New York, NY: Basic Books.

Vogel, D. L., Wester, S. R., Hammer, J. H., & Downing-Matibag, T. M. (2014). Referring men to seek help: The influence of gender role conflict and stigma. *Psychology of Men & Masculinity, 15*(1), 60–67. https://doi.org/10.1037/a0031761.

Walker, A. M. (2018). *The secret life of the cheating wife: Power, pragmatism, and pleasure in women's infidelity*. Lanham, MD: Lexington Books.

Weaver, J. R., Vandello, J. A., Bosson, J. K., & Burnaford, R. M. (2010). The proof is in the punch: Gender differences in perceptions of action and aggression as components of manhood. *Sex Roles, 62*(3–4), 241–251. https://doi.org/10.1007/s11199-009-9713-6.

West, C., & Zimmerman, D. H. (1987). Doing gender. *Gender and Society, 1*(2), 125–151.

Whisman, M. A., & Snyder, D. K. (2007). Sexual infidelity in a national survey of American women: Differences in prevalence and correlates as a function of method of assessment. *Journal of Family Psychology, 21*(2), 147–154. https://doi.org/10.1037/0893-3200.21.2.147.

Wiederman, M. W. (1997). Extramarital sex: Prevalence and correlates in a national survey. *The Journal of Sex Research, 34*, 167–174. https://doi.org/10.1080/00224499709551881.

Wiggins, J. D., & Lederer, D. A. (1984). Differential antecedents of infidelity in marriage. *American Mental Health Counselors Journal, 6*, 152–161.

Wike, R. (2014). *French more accepting of infidelity than people in other countries* [Press release]. Retrieved from https://www.pewresearch.org/fact-tank/2014/01/14/french-more-accepting-of-infidelity-than-other-countries/.

Wyne, K. (2018). Social media is at the center of most divorces, divorce attorney says in new book. *Newsweek*.

Yarob, P. E., Allgeier, E. R., & Sensibaugh, C. C. (1998). Looking deeper: Extradyadic behaviors, jealousy, and perceived unfaithfulness in hypothetical dating relationships. *Personal Relationships, 6*, 305–316. https://doi.org/10.1111/j.1475-6811.1999.tb00194.x.

Yoo, H., Bartle-Haring, S., Day, R. D., & Gangamma, R. (2014). Couple communication, emotional and sexual intimacy, and relationship satisfaction. *Journal of Sex and Marital Therapy, 40*(4), 275–293. https://doi.org/10.1080/0092623X.2012.751072.

2

Researcher Seeks Cheating Husbands: Recruiting a Closeted Population

Every study is born from a thought—however stray—that grows into a big idea, and this study is no exception. My interest in looking at the practice of infidelity grew from my longstanding ritual of reading the news online every morning. Since the algorithms of online news sources often tailor the news you see to your personal interests, my assortment of headlines often includes stories about relationships, love, marriage, and, yes, cheating.

This study did not come into being from my reading of a single story, but rather a couple of stories read over roughly six months. Like many people, I thought I had some "common sense" understandings of infidelity, but these stories challenged those assumptions. It began with coverage of two non-academic surveys. A dating site called *Undercoverlovers* found that among those who responded to their survey (presumably members of the site) 83% of men who cheated were not discovered by their partners (compared to 95% of women). I had been previously convinced by the plethora of stories of folks caught cheating that most people who cheat were eventually caught. So, I took notice of this article.

© The Author(s) 2020
A. M. Walker, *Chasing Masculinity*,
https://doi.org/10.1007/978-3-030-49818-4_2

Another site specializing in cheating, *Victoria Milan*, reported that their survey showed that 69% of their members were not cheating to shop for a new spouse, but intended to remain in their marriage. This raised my eyebrow as well. Among the popular notions about affairs is that people enter into them because on some level they want a "way out" of their marriage. I put down my breakfast plate and said aloud, "Well, then what *is* going on? What are cheaters really trying to accomplish?" Thus, the seeds of this project were planted.

In any study, figuring out where to find participants is a key concern. This study was no different. Once I had the idea and the design, I had to find men who would be willing to talk about their experiences. By its nature, participation in infidelity functions as covert. The secrecy inherent to a closeted population complicates its recruitment. There exists no directory or sampling frame from which a researcher can draw a truly random sample. I eventually remembered having read an article in a popular women's magazine about a website called *Ashley Madison*, a niche dating site aimed at married people who desire outside partners. I contacted the company via email to ask if they would be willing to post a study call on their site. And then I waited.

What Is *Ashley Madison*?

Given the massive amounts of attention directed at *Ashley Madison*, it's likely you've at least heard of the website. Its founder, Noel Biderman, has been featured on numerous articles, talk shows, and radio shows discussing the site and its aims, and a steady stream of headlines followed in the wake of the now infamous hack of the site. However, when I first began my inquiry, no one seemed to have any idea what *Ashley Madison* was—or at least they didn't want to admit to knowing. But these days, I never seem to have to clarify. Now when I talk about this project and *Ashley Madison,* I get sly looks, nervous giggles, and wry smiles. While you likely have some familiarity with the site as a concept, you may still be murky on its details.

Public fascination with *Ashley Madison* in the United States is ample—unsurprising since we're captivated by cheating generally. Google the company's name and you'll find pages upon pages of returns. There exist interviews, articles, videos, editorials, forums and discussion boards, and *Wikipedia* entries to help guide you. Magazines and newspapers have run numerous articles featuring reporters going "undercover" in an attempt to understand the mindset of *Ashley Madison* users. Site users quickly report profiles where someone identifies themselves as a reporter trying to get interviews, so going undercover is one of the few ways for journalists to actually talk with members. Reporters regale us with meets with *Ashley Madison* users in hopes of learning their motivations for using the site. They usually end with an anti-climactic declaration of them as simply "lonely."

The story of the creation of *Ashley Madison* is much like the story of any successful company's origin: someone got an idea that turned out to be a multi-million-dollar concept. After reading that nearly a third of people claiming a "single" relationship status on traditional dating sites are in reality married, Noel Biderman thought, What if these folks had a place to go online that catered to *their* interests? His reasoning: at the very least, they wouldn't be on traditional dating sites breaking the hearts of unaware singles as well as finding affair partners in dangerous venues (e.g., at the workplace) (Weigel, 2012). I know what you're thinking: *What did his wife think of this idea?* Well, she loved it so much, she even posed for the billboard ads (Borresen & Wong, 2013). With her support, he enlisted the help of his business partner, Darren Morgenstern, and together they built the *Ashley Madison* empire.

The philosophy of the company is simple. They contend that a certain portion of people will participate in outside partnerships. Lacking a venue specifically for extramarital dating, those folks wind up on traditional dating websites preying on unwitting single people. And the facts are on their side. We know that married folks have used traditional dating sites to play around while pretending to be single. We've all heard the horror stories. Launched in 2001, the site's slogan is "Life is short. Have an affair." In the spirit of "if you build it, they will come," the site hosts a reported more than 60 million members in 50 countries. The knee-jerk response of lots of people claims the site *encourages* cheating. Public forums beleaguer the original CEO, Biderman, but his stance remains that no site or commercial will induce someone to cheat. Again, the data supports this conclusion. Infidelity didn't begin with the advent of online spaces to facilitate it. The reality is: people don't really need a *reason* to cheat. Lots of folks need only a willing partner.

Not everyone took kindly to this argument. If you caught any of Noel's talk show appearances, then you also saw both the shows' hosts and guests directing their scorn and contempt straight at the site's founder. In reality, this has only added to *Ashley Madison*'s brand recognition. But for those folks living lives of quiet and private desperation—those who are desperate to remain married *and* desperate for sexual release—*Ashley Madison* is a godsend, a beacon in the dark.

How Does *Ashley Madison* Work?

Like many dating sites, membership requirements vary by gender. Specifically, women who join the site do so for free, so long as their romantic interests are men. On *Ashley Madison*, you may search for same-sex partners or you may search for other-sex partners, but you must choose. If you're a woman on the site, searching for same-sex partners requires the purchase of a membership. Men who join the site must purchase a membership package regardless. Those packages vary in price and access.

You may think it seems unfair to charge men to use the site, but not women seeking other-sex partners. Perhaps it is. However, the reasoning for this policy roots in the fact that men tend to outnumber women in online dating venues. This is even more the case on sites such as *Adult Friend Finder* and *Ashley Madison*. The free membership extended to women seeking other-sex partners serves as an enticement to draw in more female members.

While the data collection for the present study took place, the site offered an "Affair Guarantee" package, which offers (as the name suggests) a money-back guarantee for men who fail to secure an outside partner. (Collecting on this money-back guarantee requires the meeting of specific guidelines with regard to frequency of contact and number of contacts attempted.) This package confers 1000 credits to the purchaser, unlimited mail messages, and the ability to send their messages marked "priority." The member pays $249. Compare this with the "Elite" package and the "Introductory" package. The Elite grants the user 500 credits at the cost of $149, and the Introductory gives 100 credits for $49. The credits come into play as each message costs 5 credits. If a female member messages you, reading the messages costs 5 credits. Without an Affair Guarantee package, marking your message as "priority" costs 5 credits. Online dating spaces tend to function by the same gendered dating norms we observe in real life: men do most of the initiating of messages. (*Bumble* is the obvious exception to this, as that app requires women to message first.)

Profiles often display pictures carefully cropped or edited to conceal any clues to the person's identity. Members often exercise the option to curate a private gallery of more revealing pictures, which require a "key" to access. Much of the initial contact between members includes key requests and exchanges. Given the importance of anonymity on the site, these measures help grant peace of mind. Members can send "gifts," which can run up to 50 credits. Instant online messaging costs men 30 credits for 30 minutes, the minimum amount of time you can be billed. If a man wants mobile access to the site, he must cough up another $19. Mobile access reduces his chances of being caught by a spouse.

No statistics exist on the average number of women a male member must contact before even getting a face-to-face meeting. However, the men I spoke with indicated that purchasing the cheapest membership is unlikely to result in an affair. Many reported renewing their memberships several times before securing a promising outside partner. For context, many traditional dating sites are free. But even when we compare the most popular fee-based dating sites, *Ashley Madison* stacks up as expensive. *Match.com* costs $42 a month. And the Cadillac of traditional dating sites, *eHarmony.com*, runs $60 a month, but aims at finding members a spouse. Also, your membership on those sites grants you access to all site services, and both men and women must purchase memberships.

Given the high cost of *Ashley Madison* memberships, we must assume membership is skewed socioeconomically—at least for men. According to one source, the site is heavily skewed educationally; 74% of the members have a bachelor's degree (Ehrenfreund, 2014). Although many people assume that *Ashley Madison*'s membership is heavily skewed male (and in fact some people claim there are no women on the site), their membership ratio of men to women in the United States is 1–1.05 as verified by Ernst & Young in 2018.

Sampling

At the time I contacted *Ashley Madison*, I was a graduate student. My expectation was that they would simply ignore my email altogether. Imagine my delight and surprise when roughly twenty-four hours later a representative responded to my email saying that they'd be happy to assist me with advertising my study call. With their assistance, a study was born.

The full data collection included both a survey and interviews with both men and women. (The female interview data resulted in a previous book on this topic called *The Secret Life of the Cheating Wife: Power, Pragmatism, and Pleasure in Women's Infidelity*.) The survey data have featured in academic journal articles (A. Walker, 2018b). This book, however, focuses solely on the interviews with the men using the site to find outside partners. *Ashley Madison* sent emails to sectors of their membership containing a link to my survey and my email address for interviews. The survey itself also contained an invitation to interview. Both the survey and the email invitation provided a brief explanation of the study's aims and purposes, and guaranteed total confidentiality. The sample included in the present study is limited to members from the United States.

In total, the qualitative portion of this study included a total of 92 participants completing interviews. Of those, 46 were male participants. Another 28 people (9 men and 19 women) initiated interviews but dropped out without notice midway through the interview process. I utilized only the 46 complete male interviews in data analysis. The number of participants in any qualitative study is guided by achieving saturation, which refers to acquiring "data from different participants, various contexts, and various circumstances and situations—that are similar and fit within the same category" (Meadows & Morse, 2001, p. 192). This means the researcher continues to enroll and interview participants until the data collected begin to overlap or become repetitive. In this study, saturation was reached at 32, but the final sample size is 46. Data collection continued because I had already begun to interview the additional men at the point I realized saturation had occurred. Generally speaking, the researcher considers saturation reached at the point where enough information exists to replicate the study, when new information has been obtained, and when continuing to code the data is no longer viable (Fusch & Ness, 2015; Guest, Bunce, & Johnson, 2006; O'Reilly & Parker, 2013; J. Walker, 2012). Sample sizes in qualitative studies tend to remain small, and recommendations for sample sizes in qualitative studies are much smaller than for quantitative studies: 30–50 participants (Moore, 1994), and 30–60 (Bernard, 2000). For grounded theory specifically, Creswell (1998) suggests 20–30 (Cresswell, 1998). A team of researchers found that "saturation occurred within the first twelve interviews, although basic elements for metathemes were present as early as six interviews" (Guest et al., 2006, p. 59). Thus, the final sample $n = 46$ is well within the bounds of suggestions by experts in the field of qualitative inquiry. Overall, the goal is to generate a sample that is both thick (a lot of data) and rich (quality data) because ultimately saturation is about depth of the data rather than the number of participants (Burmeister & Aitken, 2012). This sample is both thick and rich.

Protection of the Research Participants

Each participant received an electronic copy of their informed consent approved by University of Kentucky's Institutional Review Board. I offered everyone the option for email or phone interview; all of the participants opted for email interviews. Given that their vetting processes and most of their contact with their outside partners occurred over email and text, email interviewing granted them more assurance of confidentiality. Participants dismissed phone interviews as an option, citing difficulty finding the privacy to speak about these experiences on the phone, concerns about being overheard, and having to explain the number if their primary partner were to see it on the bill. Others pointed out the possibility of someone searching *my* phone records in an effort to identify my participants once the study was published. Despite their privacy concerns, most of the participants eventually shared pictures of themselves, as well as other personally identifying information with me (e.g., workplace names, their real names, etc.) at some point during the interviews.

As a methodology, email interviewing grants the researcher the ability to gather interview data over a larger geographical distance than face-to-face interviews. Thus, this study includes participants from across the nation. Another benefit of this methodology includes the self-produced transcript, which negates the need for a transcriptionist. (That also meant no one but the researcher saw the transcripts, which further protected participants' anonymity.) Because email interviewing permits asynchronous scheduling, more participants can participate. Further, asynchronous email interviewing "protect[s] people who reveal sensitive personal experiences and events without them 'losing face'" (Ratislavová & Ratislav, 2014, p. 454). Additionally, a 2014 study found that asynchronous email interviewing may provide a therapeutic effort, so that participants feel heard and cared for (Ratislavová & Ratislav, 2014). McDermott and Roen (2012) found that when researching closeted or marginalized populations, this methodology provided "access to insights that might not emerge through face-to-face interviews" (McDermott & Roen, 2012, p. 560).

However, email interviewing requires an unusual skillset as many interviews occur concurrent to one another. This requires skillful navigation of email functions and internet slang to convey tone. The researcher must also juggle multiple participants, keeping one straight from another. The sense of anonymity granted the participant serves as another benefit of email interviewing (Bowker & Tuffin, 2004; Herring, 1996; Kim, Brenner, Liang, & Asay, 2003; Mann & Stewart, 2000; Matheson, 1992; Tidwell & Walther, 2002). For studies investigating closeted behaviors, this is an enormous benefit. In this study, the anonymity the participants felt contributed to their willingness to participate. In a study regarding closeted behaviors, confidentiality takes on an even larger priority. I previously successfully conducted a pilot study using email interviews, and thus felt confident to use this methodology (A. Walker, 2014a, 2014b).

I stored the data collected for this study on a password-protected, private computer to which no one else had access. Once I transferred the participant's transcript to a document identified only by a pseudonym, I deleted the actual emails. I saved participant email addresses identified by their assigned pseudonym in an Excel spreadsheet. Each participant opted for an anonymous email account for our interviews, so they cannot be identified by those email addresses.

As a methodology, online recruitment and email interviewing keep gaining popularity. Other researchers also recruited solely from websites, and then conducted the entirety of their study online (Mohebati et al., 2012; Ramo, Hall, & Prochaska, 2010; Siegel, DiLoreto, Johnson, Fortunato, & Dejong, 2011; A. Walker, 2014a, 2014b). Previous research demonstrates that email interviewing permits participants to reveal more honest information than when they are interviewed face-to-face (Bowker & Tuffin, 2004; Kim et al., 2003). The men who participated in this study were eager to share their experiences and perceptions. They were pleased to be given a voice.

The Hack

You likely remember that in July 2015, an anonymous group known as "The Impact Team" hacked *Ashley Madison*, and threatened to release the personally identifying information of the membership base unless the website yielded to their demands. Between August 18 and 20, the group leaked the data of 30 million users onto the "dark web." For any user paying for a membership, the release included their real names, addresses, credit card transactions, and search histories. While the average person has no access to the "dark web," sites showed up all over the internet allowing you to check for email addresses among those released. Capitalizing on the potential for stigma, destroyed families, and shame, extortionists contacted members with demands. A number of members committed suicide rather than face the fallout. One researcher referred to the actions of the hackers, who claimed a religious motivation, as cyberterrorism (Egloff, 2018).

Unlike the roughly 15,000 members who tied their membership to.gov and work addresses, my participants used anonymous emails to join the site. Thus, the hack didn't impact them. The then-CEO, Noel Biderman, was not so lucky. The hack revealed at least three attempts on his part to have affairs using the site. He stepped down as CEO of *Ashley Madison*. He wasn't the only one: many members of management resigned. At present, the company operates with a senior leadership team rather than a CEO. *Ashley Madison* continues to thrive. Its U.S. membership alone increased by 16.7%. Some folks don't understand why anyone would risk membership on the site given the previous hack. As it turns out, the hack and its fallout don't stack up against human sexual need. Married desperation still exists, and *Ashley Madison* is still there to help. However, the ability of the site to endure sparked much interest. In fact, Karen Robson and Leyland Pitt wrote a book aimed at business students using the hack and its aftermath—including what the authors call "rebranding"—as a case study (Robson & Pitt, 2018). Other researchers considered the ethical questions around using data from the company in research (Seigfried-Spellar, 2015).

Bots

At the time of the hack, another controversy dogged *Ashley Madison* and other dating sites: the use of bots. Specifically, some alleged that many dating sites employed the use of both fake profiles of women and bots, which sent fake messages to male members, in an effort to draw in and retain paying members. This concern remains prevalent and articles exist to help individuals discern bots from real members based on their patterns of behavior (e.g., *Medium*'s "Spot the Bot" article). Online discussion boards feature conversations between users who believe certain sites are primarily bots (e.g., *Quora*'s discussion of *Plenty of Fish*). Although plenty of individuals still employ dating apps and sites, concerns about fake profiles and bots abound.

In 2015, *Gizmodo* published Annalee Newitz's article which alleged that on *Ashley Madison*, at most, real women accounted for 12,000 of the profiles. *Ashley Madison* rejected the claim, as did users of the site. The site also criticized Newitz's methodology, explaining that she misunderstood much of what she'd seen. Newitz then retracted her initial claim and acknowledged that her estimate of the real women on the site was low. She took another look at the data and published an update titled "*Ashley Madison* Code Shows More Women and More Bots" which claimed the site had over 70,000 such bots. She further explained that the dump from the Impact Team revealed "hundreds of readable company emails that revealed the company was paying people to create fake women's profiles and to chat with men on the site" (Newitz, 2015). Newitz claimed the code for the bots appeared to go back to mid-2010.

By 2016, *Ashley Madison* admitted to the use of bots to entice memberships. However, they stated that they discontinued use of the bot program in late 2015. In fact, the company explained that prior to the hack, they had already begun the process of shutting the program down. To verify its discontinuance, in 2017 *Ashley Madison* brought in Ernst & Young to both verify their membership numbers and the absence of a bot program. The report confirmed that the site hosts millions of men and women, and has stopped using bots.

Limitations

While email interviewing provides many benefits, there are limitations. Interviewing via email requires a higher level of motivation and interest in the interview itself on the part of the participant (Chen & Hinton, 1999; Meho, 2006). The typing and reading required can be physically demanding. While the asynchronous nature eliminates scheduling issues, it requires extra time due to the reading, thinking, typing, and maintaining a thread throughout responses. Given the concurrent nature of email interviewing, the researcher must get a response onto the screen while simultaneously probing participant responses, keeping everyone engaged and involved, and asking all relevant questions. Denoting emotion and intonation through emoticons and acronyms requires the researcher's familiarity. A marked limitation of this methodology includes the lack of visual cues on the part of both participant and researcher. Email interviews lack the benefit of body language to help discern meaning and intent.

Email interviews can take weeks to complete. That longer timeframe sometimes results in participant frustration, loss of interest, and drop-out (Hodgson, 2004). Inadvertent delivery to spam or clutter folders thwart interviews. Cluttered and highly trafficked email accounts result in lost interview questions. Sometimes participants read interviewer emails, but forget to respond. Online data collection necessitates computer access and literacy, which excludes certain groups. However, in this study, individuals well-versed in online communication served as the target population.

Given this is a qualitative project, we cannot generalize the results to larger populations on a statistical basis. However, "statistical-probability generalization is neither applicable to qualitative research nor a goal of it" (Smith, 2018, p. 140). Qualitative methods produce data reflective of shared experiences and meanings. The findings reveal culturally and socially shaped experiences. The point of qualitative research is "examining people's lives in rich detail" which is accomplished through talking with "small numbers of people" "often chosen through purposive or purposeful sampling strategies" (Smith, 2018, p. 140). Thus, the small sample sizes utilized in qualitative studies function not as a weakness, but as a strength of the methodology, enabling the researcher to offer rich insights into human experience (Braun & Clarke, 2013; Smith, 2018; Sparkes & Smith, 2014). However, qualitative work often offers a type of generalizability called transferability, which is accomplished "when the readers feel as though the story of the research overlaps with their own situation and they intuitively transfer the research to their own action" (Tracy, 2010, p. 845). According to Tracy (2010), researchers create transferability through "gathering direct testimony, providing rich description, and writing accessibly and invitationally" (Tracy, 2010, p. 845). Thus, the purpose of this study isn't to suggest that the findings represent *all* men, or even all men participating in outside partnerships. However, readers may see themselves in these narratives, or gain more understanding of the experiences and perceptions of men who intentionally sought an outside partner online.

Personal Identities of the Researcher

Because I am a woman, I initially had concerns that my gender might limit men's willingness to talk with me openly. Thankfully, men eagerly shared their stories. However, my gender did impact some facets of the interviews, as I note in the text. Specifically, men repeatedly reiterated their own sexual prowess. Had I been a man, the participants may not have felt so compelled to make mention of this. However, given that masculinity is something bestowed upon him by others rather than something he can pronounce of himself (Michniewicz, Vandello, & Bosson, 2014), participants may have felt just as obliged to make sure a male researcher understood them as sexually competent.

Previous research has investigated the ways gender may come to bear upon qualitative interviews; however, as noted by Sallee and Harris (2011) "opportunities for cross-gender interviews may lead to richer responses from participants" (Sallee & Harris, 2011, p. 426). Specifically, the authors found that some men may be "more introspective about masculinities in their interviews with the female researcher, simply because they did not feel the need to live up to masculine expectations" (Sallee & Harris, 2011, p. 426). Further, the authors posited that talking with a female researcher may in fact permit at least some participants to "engage in thoughtful reflection about masculinities" (Sallee & Harris, 2011, p. 426). However, gender must still be considered here because male participants may have "exaggerated their masculine behavior" (Sallee & Harris, 2011, p. 426). Ultimately, Sallee and Harris resolved that we cannot know whether gender impacts "truthful" responses. We can only be cognizant of its possible role. They determined that "participants may simply have played up different aspects of their identities" (Sallee & Harris, 2011, p. 427).

The specific social statuses of the interviewer come to bear on interactions with participants, just as they do in all arenas of our lives. As a team led by Patrick Jachyra in 2014 found, "both individual and structural social variables can influence the data in unpredictable ways" (Jachyraa, Atkinsona, & Gibson, 2014, p. 569). Thus, reflexivity about my own social statuses must be considered in terms of their impact on data collection. I am a white, middle-aged woman, who has a history of romantic relationships with men. Those statuses cannot be ignored as they undoubtedly play a role. The fact that I collected data remotely may have mitigated some of those effects. After all, we were never face-to-face, which may have made it possible for interviewees to at times "forget" my particular statuses. However, it's also certainly possible that my gender and race remained salient for participants throughout our conversations. Additionally, my statuses certainly shape my lens of the world and the men's narratives. Ultimately, in qualitative research, the "interviewer and interviewee co-construct the data" together while carting our histories, perceptions, biases, and identities into that interview (Eggly, 2002; Jachyraa et al., 2014, p. 569).

In the end, qualitative interviews exist as a snapshot of the participant's perceptions of their experiences in that moment. An interview conducted at another time or by another interviewer might yield a different perspective. If I interviewed these participants again in a year, 5 years, or a decade, their perspectives would likely shift, especially depending upon how they felt their participation in outside partnerships played out.

Data Collection and Analysis

Due to the nature of recruitment for this project, new participants came in waves correlated to the website's email blasts. So, I conducted semi-structured interviews concurrent to one another throughout the study. The interviews functioned as a conversation as I sent out one question at a time. When the participant responded, I asked any follow-up questions before posing the next question in the protocol. The nature of this approach empowers the participant to share their experiences in their own words and in their own way. They shared many details and stories of their lives and experiences, which they felt relevant to their own meaning-making or simply felt inclined to share. The more the conversation is driven by the participant's desire to share, the more likely the data include those experiences the man himself regards as both influential and important in his relationship and sexual life.

The average transcript was more than six single-spaced pages long, and the longest transcript in this study was 14 single-spaced pages. Thirteen percent of the transcripts were 10 single-spaced pages or longer. A single interview often took weeks to accomplish, giving the participants time to consider their response to my questions. Many times, the participant would say things such as, "I got really off topic there" or "I don't know why I just shared since that wasn't really what you asked, but hopefully you understand me better." Occasionally, a participant responded to a question with a request for time to think about the question before responding.

The process of analysis required unpacking and weaving back together aspects of the data that yielded information about the men's realities of their primary partnerships and their outside partnerships. The method of data analysis employed here was grounded theory, which utilizes the constant comparative method credited to Glaser and Strauss (1967). With grounded theory, the researcher inductively analyzes data to understand the lived experiences of the participants. The researcher approaches the research without a hypothesis regarding the phenomenon in question. Rather than going into the study itself with a predetermined theory concerning what is happening, the data itself guides the researcher's theory formation (Corbin & Strauss, 1998; Glaser & Strauss, 1967).

Using this methodology, a repetitive comparison of concepts, themes, and experiences both between and within data sets is utilized (Merriam, 1998, 2002). In grounded theory, data analysis is conducted in distinct phases (Corbin & Strauss, 1998) as data are analyzed on several levels, including data description, category construction, and making inferences to explain the phenomenon in question (Creswell, 1998). I reviewed transcript documents line-by-line and allocated to develop themes and patterns that gave shape to the data. This coding, conceptualizing, and categorizing took place by hand, which provided the means of "distilling large quantities of information to uncover significant features and elements that are embedded in the data" (Stringer, 2007, p. 95).

Qualitative methods produce data that are reflective of shared experiences and meanings. The findings reflect experiences that are culturally and socially shaped. The results of grounded theory analysis can provide us with insight into social norms, but the shared nature of these meanings and experiences limit our ability to isolate which influences are sociocultural and which are individual (Rothe, 2000). This methodology permitted the researcher to discern the meaning-making of the men in the study and to examine their experiences and contributions to the knowledge we have regarding men's experiences with infidelity. I hope the result offers richly textured insights into the nature and meanings of these men's extramarital and marital lives.

Who Are These Men?

The men who participated in this study ranged in age from 27 to 70 years of age. The average age was 45.9. Thirty percent (14) of the participants were between the ages of 40–49. Another 26% (12) of the sample ranged in age from 30 to 39. Only three participants fell on the youngest end of the spectrum: 27–29; and only two fell on the oldest end of the spectrum: 70. Fifteen percent of the participants (7) fell into ages 50–59, and another 15% (7) into the 60–69 category. Forty of the participants were White; only six men of color participated. Only one man who either self-identified as bisexual or reported same-sex sexual encounters participated. While *Ashley Madison* does permit searching for same-sex partners, such memberships are not free, and the pool of potential partners on the site is quite small. These men reported from across the United States. Nearly all of the men described themselves as married. Only three were single, but partnered. Three men were divorced with a primary partner. All but two men in the sample expressed a clear desire to remain in their primary partnership. Those men stated openly they wanted to exit their primary relationships at some point in the future, but were not ready to do so at present or the foreseeable future. Thirty-one of the men (67%) explicitly mentioned having children at some point during the interview. One-third (15) of the men in this sample stated they were either virgins or inexperienced sexually at the time they entered into their marriages.

Why Are These Men Cheating?

As a culture, we think we have men's infidelity figured out. The narratives that "men are dogs" and "all men have cheated/will cheat given the opportunity" remain prevalent in our society. In terms of men and cheating, we take a dim view. We assume men cheat because they simply cannot resist the draw of a "new" partner, or they simply lack self-control. The prevailing discussions regarding men's infidelity paint them with a broad and unflattering brush.

The men in this study reported a sense of emasculation provoked by their perception of the dynamics within their primary partnerships as their primary motivation for participation in outside partnerships. Thirty-seven men (80%) in the study described unsatisfying primary partnerships, which lacked adequate amounts of validation and attention. Like roughly half of women in the previous sample, who reported a sexless marriage (while many more reported their marriages orgasmless), thirty-five men (76%) in the sample reported being in a sexless marriage. Yet while the bulk of the women in my previous book sought to outsource the sexual aspect of their marriage, these men spoke more about the pain of the loss of relational management, validation, and emotional support. This difference lies not in gender, but in the dynamics of their primary partnerships. Like the seven women in the previous book, who sought to outsource the emotional aspect of their primary partnerships to sexual outside partners, the men in this inquiry did as well. Thus, the difference between the women reporting sexless and orgasmless primary partnerships, who sought to outsource the sexual aspect of their primary partnerships to an interested third party, and the men in sexless marriages in this inquiry seeking to outsource the emotional aspect of their primary partnerships exists in their emotional bonds at home. The women reporting sexless/orgasmless primary partnerships also reported strong relationships with their partners at home. They spoke of being good friends, mutual respect, and caring. The men in this inquiry in these sexless primary partnerships failed to describe them similarly. Their descriptions mirrored the reports of the seven women in the previous book whose primary partnerships functioned as extremely emotionally unsatisfying. Thus, this functions not as a gender difference, so much as a difference in primary partner dynamics. Contrary to our current "common sense" positioning of men's infidelity and the gendered nature of infidelity, the men in this sample challenge many of our current assumptions about cheating—just as the women's accounts did. (Note: for clarity, men regarded their primary partners with the same fondness as the bulk of the women in my previous study. It was their descriptions of those primary relationships that differed.)

Decision to Cheat

Despite the deep-seated insecurities fed by the dynamics of the sexual nature of their primary partnerships, and their upset at the loss of relational management, men failed to make the decision to engage in an affair lightly. Every man in this inquiry talked about the circumstances that led to their leap into infidelity. Sloan (36, married) explained:

> I didn't decide to pursue an outside relationship on a whim. It definitely took a lot of soul searching. And although the stereotype of a guy who has an affair is someone who is a heartless ass, who doesn't care if he hurts his wife, I feel like I'm the complete opposite of that.

For these men, primary partnerships failed to offer the love and affection expected. After years of enduring a relationship where their needs were not met, they decided to act. They made the decision to do so in an effort to avoid leaving. Sloan (36, married) added, "My decision to pursue an affair was actually made in hopes of preserving my marriage. I decided my marriage had too many great things about it to end things because of the lack of intimacy." The emotional toll of the loss of enthusiastic, sensual consortium, emotional support, validation, praise, and relational management in their marriages proved substantial. Riley (39, married) added:

> I think the loneliness and hopelessness just reached a point one night where I had to do something, and take whatever consequences came.

Living in my marriage any longer without emotional or physical intimacy is simply not possible. My mental and physical health are in tatters,
ravaged by depression. There became no reason to want to wake up
tomorrow. No carrot at the end of the stick, only obligations to fulfill.
Sleep was the only respite.

While it is easy for the outsider to write off the conditions of these
primary partnerships, we cannot ignore the psychological toll for the
men in this study. Research shows that satisfying intimate relationships result in better physical health (Cohen et al., 1998), the ability
to recover from illness more quickly (Kiecolt-Glaser et al., 2005), and
a longer life (Gallo, Troxel, Matthews, & Kuller, 2003; Holt-Lundstad,
Smith, & Layton, 2010). In other words, we are physically and emotionally healthier when we are in satisfying intimate relationships. Thus,
men's painful accounts of the toll of these fractured marriages reflect the
importance of healthy, happy long-term intimate pairings.

Over time, these men determined that their marriages simply could
not deliver what they needed. Greg (53, married) said, "The lack of a sex
life and emotional intimacy with my primary partner definitely was/is a
major driver in seeking an outside partner." This realization drove them
to act. At some point, the men reconciled the disparity between their
expectations of marriage and its realities. As painful as that realization
was, men made decisions to remedy their lack of sexual intimacy.

Efforts to Repair

Like the women in my previous book, before deciding to engage in an
affair, however, the men tried to fix the conditions of their marriages.
Many begged their spouse to go to therapy, or were even successful in
getting them to go. Sloan (36, married) talked about his efforts to recover
the previous level of intimacy in his marriage:

> We'd tried a lot of things to work these problems out, including coun-
> seling. Our overall relationship improved and stayed strong, but all the
> improvements in our sex life quickly disappeared with the passage of time.

These efforts left much to be desired. Mitch (59, married) said, "She just replies that she can't do what I want, doesn't know why, and then shuts down. No more discussion. I've suggested we go to counseling; she says it wouldn't change anything." Men followed the social scripts available to them with regard to managing relationships only to have those attempts fail. Riley (39, married) explained:

> Counseling and medication can only take the edge off in that situation; they cannot change the reasons for the depression and hopelessness. As the closeness and affection—[and] non-sexual affection [is just] as important as sexual—start to happen more frequently [in the outside partnership], I can begin to feel parts of myself reawaken. Things like joy, hope, peace, contentment: they bring a warmth back to life, color. Without these things, I believe divorce or suicide would have been the only alternatives.

Thus, despite their best efforts at rectifying the fissures in their primary relationship, the problems remained.

The decision to seek out an outside partner came only after sincere attempts to fix their marriages. When efforts to right the conditions in their primary partnership were unsuccessful, they could only remain patient for so long. The process of accepting that their marriages weren't going to change was often a long one. Simon (39, married) added, "The decision to pursue and participate was a long-term evolution of the feelings I felt and frustration in my existing relationship." Eventually, the men decided to stop waiting for their marriages to change, and instead changed their own circumstances. While it's certainly easy to sit in judgment of anyone who cheats, we must admit that relationships are difficult. Marriage is challenging; it's work. When one party believes they are the only one putting in the work, marriage becomes infinitely more difficult.

Cheating to Stay

For all but two of the men in this study, cheating served as a stopgap or a workaround for leaving. Forty-four of the men (96%) in this sample explicitly spoke of their desire to remain with their primary partner, but made it clear that without the relief affairs offered, they would end up exiting their primary partnerships. In this way, men's narratives echoed the sentiments of women in my book, *The Secret Life of the Cheating Wife* (A. Walker, 2018a). Like most of the women in that study, for the overwhelming majority of this sample, their descriptions of their primary partner painted a picture of tremendous love, regard, and fondness. Seth (31, married) explained, "I'm not going anywhere regardless of how extramarital trysts do or do not play out. I've built my life around her." In terms of positives their primary partners brought to the table, there were many. Kurt (33, married) described his wife:

> I have ZERO desire to get divorced. My wife and I get along great. We go to new restaurants and movies; we try new recipes, all that good stuff. We don't fight over money or bicker about housework. I love my wife very much and I know she returns the feeling.

These men were not confused by their feelings toward their primary partner. They knew these were great women. Patrick (33, married) added, "Not to mention my wife being the best mother my kids can have." In fact, for many of these men, their primary partners were nearly perfect. Bodi (32, married) said, "My relationship with my wife is outstanding. We are envied by many people." Thus, these men were clear on what their marriages were and were not. Gus (62, married) added, "My primary relationship partner is my best friend in many ways." These men valued their primary partners. Tucker (60, married) explained:

> [My outside partner and I] know that we do not desire a change in our primary partners. We are not "in love." We enjoy each other, thank each other, and go back to our lives. My wife is my best friend. I enjoy her immensely. Our personalities match well. Our goals are well aligned, as I believe are the goals of my outside partner.

We tend to imagine cheaters as people with no regard for their spouse at home, but that was not the case for the men of this study. This echoed the sentiment of the women in my previous study. Those women also spoke highly of their primary partners (A. Walker, 2018a).

No matter how perfect their primary partners, the lack of intimacy—both emotional and sexual—was an issue. Sloan stated, (36, married) "If you asked me to make a list of the qualities I want to have in a partner, my wife has almost all of them." This gap in the primary partnership created a lot of tension and inner conflict for these men. Tripp (48, married) said this:

> I once described my marriage like the old meatloaf song, "Two out of Three ain't Bad." You begin a relationship that seems to meet a lot of your needs but is lacking something, but you tell yourself you're being unrealistic, picky, selfish. [The] problem is that 3rd thing becomes a bigger issue as the years go by, until it's the elephant in the living room.

The knowledge that within their marriage existed a disparity in terms of sexual desire did not erase their feelings. Jake (48, married) added, "I remain in my present relationship because of my love and feelings for her." Part of the process that led these men to affairs included accepting their marriages and their spouses for what and whom they were.

Despite those realities, they were committed to staying. Byron (57, married) explained, "I have no plans to give up on her or on us." Nearly every man in this study made that statement. Milo (29, married) echoed that sentiment: "But I get along with her well enough, and enjoy what we have together too much not leave her." While it may seem counterintuitive for someone to cheat to stay married, that was the strategy the men employed. They made their primary partnership a priority even while carrying on affairs. Scott (40, married) explained:

> My primary relationship comes first. I don't want anything to jeopardize it, and take every precaution to keep the two relationships separate. If there's a toss-up situation where I can choose doing something for my

side relationship (meeting up, in most cases) or doing something for my primary relationship (something I've said I would get done around the house, or some other obligation I've committed to), the primary relationship comes first to keep the primary relationship strong. I can get another side relationship, given enough time and effort, but I don't want to lose my primary relationship or make it difficult.

I spend a lot of time talking about infidelity with people who ask about my research. A common response is to scoff at these people and write their actions off as "having their cake and eating it, too." The very idea of cheaters putting their marriages first seems counterintuitive. However, that's exactly what these men reported, which echoes the findings of my previous work on women participating in outside partnerships (A. Walker, 2018a).

For some men, the fact that they felt such attraction to their wives worked against them. Mitch (59, married) said:

> She is a beautiful woman, looks ten years younger than her age, and I am still very attracted to her. So, I keep coming back for more of the same. Sometimes I say to myself I'm just going to stop approaching her for sex, and see what she does, but I can't stay away from her for very long.

Men talked about resolving to stop asking their primary partners for sex in an effort to stop the pain of rejection. But their attraction to and fondness for their wives made that difficult. For other men, the disparity in sexual interest was apparent before marriage, but their pull toward their primary partner was too strong to ignore. These men married their wives as a result of immense attraction, desire, and love. The fact that the marriage failed to meet their needs didn't change that. In our culture, it's not okay to admit that we're unhappy with the sex in our monogamous relationship. That taboo doesn't change the reality that many people do in fact experience dissatisfaction within that experience.

All of the men in the study clearly stated that they were cheating in an effort to remain married (in the case of the two men who desired to eventually leave their primary partnerships, they wanted to remain within them for the time being). Mitch (59, married) said, "I doubt I would be in my primary relationship if it weren't for those other relationships."

For these men, affairs offered an outlet to get needs met. The point of these affairs was not to find another wife or to leave. Riley (39, married) added, "I am not looking to end my family. I'm looking to make sticking with my family possible by supplementing what's missing for as long as I can." Outside partnerships served to help keep men in marriages, while getting their needs met with a partner who truly desired them. Greg (53, married) echoed that sentiment: "There is a part of me that believes if I had not engaged in these OP [outside partner] activities our marriage would be over." For these men, affairs were a means to an end. For men who adored their wives but still needed intimacy and support that they weren't getting at home, outside partnerships provided an outlet. Tucker (60, married) articulated his situation: "My wife is my best friend. Close. Very easy to be affectionate. We have similar goals, are both very busy people. I credit my current OP [outside partnership] for saving my marriage." For many men, an outside partnership could take the pressure off their primary partnership to fulfill all of their needs.

Alongside men's seemingly pat responses such as "I love her," many men pointed out that "we have children together" and for them that was a reason to remain in the partnership as well. Donald (61, married) explained, "I am highly motivated to remain in this relationship. Strong family ties, as well as my love for my spouse helps me remain in this relationship." Even among the five men who reported a loss of trust in their primary partner/partnership, outside partnerships still stood second to their primary, if for no other reason than their children. Gabriel (40, married) discovered his wife's infidelity. That loss of trust led him to seek out outside partnerships of his own. He explained that despite the circumstances of his marriage, he was committed to remaining in it. He explained, "Principally, my [child] was the motivating factor for me to stay in the marriage as I had just obtained a job in another state. So, I was facing seeing my [child] only in the summer." Love for their wives and children rooted these men in their primary partnerships.

It remains possible that fully delving into those reasons might be akin to pulling on the threads of a blanket: you run the risk of unraveling the whole thing. Also, their seemingly glib answers may function as self-protection, and protection for their families—and the very fabric of their lives. Or maybe the answers really *are* that simple. While it is easy to scoff at the simplicity of these men's reasons for staying in unsatisfying primary partnerships, doing so ignores our own truths. Thinking about our own primary partnerships, what reasons would we give a stranger as to why we remain? "I love them" and concern for our children would top our lists as well. These men function no differently from us in that regard.

This group of men circumvented the typical and expected route for those who find marriage unfulfilling. Rather than divorce and begin anew with another partner, they opted for secret concurrent sexual liaisons. Untying yourself from a marriage is costly both financially and emotionally. There is much to lose. Shared financial interests and holdings are threatened. For men, concerns about access to their children play a central role here. Splitting up a marriage doesn't just upend your life, but also that of your spouse and your children. For men who still love their wives, the prospect is daunting. For men who value their close relationships with their children, the idea of living away from them can be heart-breaking. Thus, like the women in my previous book, they exercised an Infidelity Workaround, and outsourced the aspects of their marriages that failed to meet their needs to a more interested third party.

Conclusion

The purpose of this qualitative study was to explore the question, "How do men with outside partners make meaning of that experience, and how do these relationships impact their primary partnerships?" I interviewed forty-six men who generously shared their stories about participation in outside partnerships, and how they affected their primary partnerships. Semi-structured interviews provided opportunities to probe participant responses for meaning and clarity. Email interviews self-produce transcripts. Those transcripts were member-checked and re-read several times to analyze for themes.

This overwhelmingly White, married, predominantly middle-class group of men provided insight into the qualities of outside partnerships formed purposefully from online profiles for extramarital affairs. The narratives in this study illustrate men's meaning-making of their experiences seeking out and participating in outside partnerships concurrent to their primary partnerships. The existing literature on infidelity suggests distinct gender differences in approaching and navigating outside partnerships. Specifically, previous literature implies that men enter these associations solely for sexual reasons and value the sexual aspect of them more highly. The sample presented here challenges that understanding of men's participation in infidelity.

References

Bernard, H. R. (2000). *Social research methods*. Thousand Oaks, CA: Sage.

Borresen, K., & Wong, B. (2013, April 1). *Ashley Madison creator Noel Biderman talks marriage with his wife of nearly 10 years, Amanda*. Retrieved from https://www.huffpost.com/entry/ashley-madison-creator_n_2993008.

Bowker, N., & Tuffin, K. (2004). Using the online medium for discursive research about people with disabilities. *Social Science Computer Review, 22*(2), 228–241. https://doi.org/10.1177/0894439303262561.

Braun, V., & Clarke, V. (2013). *Successful qualitative research: A practical guide for beginners*. London: Sage.

Burmeister, E., & Aitken, L. M. (2012). Sample size: How many is enough? *Australian Critical Care, 25*(4), 271–274. https://doi.org/10.1016/j.aucc.2012.07.002.

Chen, P., & Hinton, S. M. (1999). Real-time interviewing using the world wide web. *Sociological Research Online, 4*(3), 63–81.

Cohen, S., Frank, E., Doyle, W. J., Skoner, D. P., Rabin, B. S., & Jack M. Gwaltney, J. (1998). Types of stressors that increase susceptibility to the common cold in healthy adults. *Health Psychology, 17*, 214–223. http://dx.doi.org/10.1037/0278-6133.17.3.214.

Corbin, J., & Strauss, A. (1998). *Basics of qualitative research: Techniques and procedures for developing grounded theory*. Thousand Oaks, CA: Sage.

Cresswell, J. (1998). *Qualitative inquiry and research design: Choosing among five traditions*. Thousand Oaks, CA: Sage.

Eggly, S. (2002). Physician-patient co-construction of illness narratives in the medical interview. *Health Communication, 14*(3), 339–360. https://doi.org/10.1207/S15327027HC1403_3.

Egloff, F. J. (2018). *Let's talk cyberterrorism—An academic assessment*. Paper presented at the International Studies Association Annual Conference, San Francisco.

Ehrenfreund, M. (2014, May 1). The economics of adultery. *The Washington Post*.

Fusch, P. I., & Ness, L. R. (2015). *Are we there yet? Data saturation in qualitative research*. Retrieved from http://www.nova.edu/ssss/QR/QR20/9/fusch1.pdf.

Gallo, L. C., Troxel, W. M., Matthews, K. A., & Kuller, L. H. (2003). Marital status and quality in middle-aged women: Associations with levels and trajectories of cardiovascular risk factors. *Health Psychology, 22,* 453–463. https://doi.org/10.1037/0278-6133.22.5.453.

Glaser, B. G., & Strauss, A. (1967). *The discovery of grounded theory: Strategies for qualitative research*. Chicago, IL: Aldine Publishing Co.

Guest, G., Bunce, A., & Johnson, L. (2006). How many interviews are enough? An experiment with data saturation and variability. *Field Methods, 18*(1), 59–82. https://doi.org/10.1177/1525822X05279903.

Herring, S. C. (1996). *Computer-mediated communication: Linguistic, social and cross-cultural perspectives*. Philadelphia, PA: John Benjamin Publishing Company.

Hodgson, S. (2004). Cutting through the silence: A sociological construction of self-injury. *Sociological Inquiry, 74*(2), 162–179. https://doi.org/10.1111/j.1475-682X.2004.00085.x.

Holt-Lundstad, J., Smith, T. B., & Layton, J. B. (2010). Social relationships and mortality risk: A meta-analytic review. *PLoS Medicine, 7*(7), e100316. https://doi.org/10.1371/journal.pmed.1000316.

Jachyraa, P., Atkinsona, M., & Gibson, B. E. (2014). Gender performativity during interviews with adolescent boys. *Qualitative Research in Sport, Exercise and Health, 6*(4), 568–582. https://doi.org/10.1080/2159676X.2013.877960.

Kiecolt-Glaser, J. K., Loving, T. J., Stowell, J. R., Malarkey, W. B., Lemeshow, S., Dickinson, S. L., & Glaser, R. (2005). Hostile marital interactions, proinflammatory cytokine production, and wound healing. *Archives of General Psychiatry, 62,* 1377–1384. http://dx.doi.org/10.1001/archpsyc.62.12.1377.

Kim, B. S., Brenner, B. R., Liang, C. T. H., & Asay, P. A. (2003). A qualitative study of adaptation experiences of 1.5-generation Asian Americans *Cultural Diversity & Ethnic Minority Psychology, 9*(2), 156–170. https://doi.org/10.1037/1099-9809.9.2.156.

Mann, C., & Stewart, F. (2000). *Internet communication and qualitative research: A handbook for researching online.* London: Sage.

Matheson, K. (1992). Women and computer technology: Communicating for herself. In M. Lea (Ed.), *Contexts of computer-mediated communication* (pp. 66–88). Hemel Hempstead: Harvester Wheatsheaf.

McDermott, E., & Roen, K. (2012). Youth on the virtual edge: Researching marginalized sexualities and genders online. *Qualitative Health Research, 22*(4), 560–570. https://doi.org/10.1177/1049732311425052.

Meadows, L. M., & Morse, J. M. (2001). Constructing evidence within the qualitative project. In J. M. Morse, J. M. Swanson, & A. J. Kuzel (Eds.), *The nature of evidence in qualitative inquiry* (pp. 187–200). Newbury Park, CA: Sage.

Meho, L. I. (2006). E-mail interviewing in qualitative research: A methodological discussion: Research articles. *Journal of the American Society for Information Science and Technology, 57*(10), 1284–1295. https://doi.org/10.1002/asi.v57:10.

Merriam, S. B. (1998). *Qualitative research and case study applications in education.* San Francisco, CA: Jossey-Bass.

Merriam, S. B. (2002). *Qualitative research in practice: Examples for discussion and analysis.* San Francisco, CA: Jossey-Bass.

Michniewicz, K. S., Vandello, J. A., & Bosson, J. K. (2014). Men's (mis) perceptions of the gender threatening consequences of unemployment. *Sex Roles, 7*(3–4), 88–97. https://doi.org/10.1007/s11199-013-0339-3.

Mohebati, A., Knutson, A., Zhou, X. K., Smith, J. J., Brown, P. H., Dannenberg, A. J., & Szabo, E. (2012). A web-based screening and accrual strategy for a cancer prevention clinical trial in healthy smokers. *Contemporary Clinical Trials, 33*(5), 942–948. http://dx.doi.org/10.1016/j.cct.2012.07.004.

Moore, J. M. (1994). Designing funded qualitative research. In N. K. Denzin & Y. S. Lincoln (Eds.), *Handbook of qualitative research* (pp. 220–235). Thousand Oaks, CA: Sage.

Newitz, A. (2015, August 31). Ashley Madison Code Shows more women and more bots. *Gizmodo.*

O'Reilly, M., & Parker, N. (2013). Unsatisfactory saturation: A critical exploration of the notion of saturated sample sizes in qualitative research. *Qualitative Research, 13*(2), 190–197. https://doi.org/10.1177/1468794112446106.

Ramo, D. E., Hall, S. M., & Prochaska, J. J. (2010). Reaching young adult smokers through the internet: Comparison of three recruitment mechanisms. *Nicotine & Tobacco Research, 12*(7), 768–775. https://doi.org/10. 1093/ntr/ntq086.

Ratislavová, K., & Ratislav, J. (2014). Asynchronous email interview as a qualitative research method in the humanities. *Human Affairs, 24*(4), 452–460. https://doi.org/10.2478/s13374-014-0240-y.

Robson, K., & Pitt, L. (2018). *Internet vigilantism and Ashley Madison: Rebranding after a cyberattack*. London: Sage.

Rothe, P. J. (2000). *Undertaking qualitative research: Concepts and cases in injury, health and social life*. Edmonton, AB: The University of Alberta Press.

Sallee, M. W., & Harris, F. (2011). Gender performance in qualitative studies of masculinities. *Qualitative Research, 11*(4), 409–429. https://doi.org/10. 1177/1468794111404322.

Seigfried-Spellar, K. C. (2015). *Analyzing the Ashley Madison dataset?* Paper presented at the Dawn or Doom Purdue University.

Siegel, M., DiLoreto, J., Johnson, A., Fortunato, E. K., & Dejong, W. (2011). Development and pilot testing of an internet-based survey instrument to measure the alcohol brand preferences of U.S. youth. *Alcoholism-Clinical and Experimental Research, 35*(4), 765–772. https://doi.org/10.1111/j.1530-0277.2010.01394.x.

Smith, B. (2018). Generalizability in qualitative research: Misunderstandings, opportunities and recommendations for the sport and exercise sciences. *Qualitiative Research in Sport, 10*(1), 137–149. https://doi.org/10.1080/215 9676X.2017.1393221.

Sparkes, A. C., & Smith, B. (2014). *Qualitative research methods in sport, exercise and health: From process to product*. New York, NY: Routledge/Taylor & Francis Group.

Stringer, E. T. (2007). *Action research*. London: Sage.

Tidwell, L. C., & Walther, J. B. (2002). Computer-mediated communication effects on disclosure, impressions, and interpersonal evaluations: Getting to know one another a bit at a time. *Human Communication Research, 28*(3), 317–348. https://doi.org/10.1111/j.1468-2958.2002.tb00811.x.

Tracy, S. J. (2010). Qualitative quality: Eight "Big-Tent" criteria for excellent qualitative research. *Qualitative Inquiry, 16*(10), 837–851. https://doi.org/ 10.1177/1077800410383121.

Walker, A. M. (2014a). "I'm not a lesbian; I'm just a freak": A pilot study of the experiences of women in assumed-monogamous other-sex unions seeking secret same-sex encounters online, their negotiation of sexual desire, and meaning-making of sexual identity. *Sexuality and Culture, 18*(4), 911–935. https://doi.org/10.1007/s12119-014-9226-5.

Walker, A. M. (2014b). 'Our little secret': How publicly heterosexual women make meaning from their 'undercover' same-sex sexual experiences. *Journal of Bisexuality, 14*(2), 194–208. https://doi.org/10.1080/15299716.2014.902347.

Walker, A. M. (2018a). *The secret life of the cheating wife: Power, pragmatism, and pleasure in women's infidelity.* Lanham, MD: Lexington Books.

Walker, A. M. (2018b). Having your cake and eating it, too: Factors impacting perception of life satisfaction during outside partnerships. *Sexuality & Culture, 23,* 112–131. https://doi.org/10.1007/s12119-018-9545-z

Walker, J. L. (2012). The use of saturation in qualitative research. *Canadian Journal of Cardiovascular Nursing, 22*(2), 37–41.

Weigel, J. (2012, February 13). Valentine's Day for cheaters. *Chicago Tribune.* Retrieved from https://www.chicagotribune.com/lifestyles/ct-tribu-weigel-mistress-day-20120214-column.html.

3

"Men Need Their Egos Pumped up Regularly": Primary Partnerships Sow the Seeds of Men's Doubt

Introduction

The men in this study reported a need for their primary partners to help manage their emotional lives. Specifically, they failed to see themselves as able to voice their feelings in the absence of their primary partner's probing. They remained reliant on her noticing their sadness and pressing them to talk about it, so that it might be addressed. I refer to these acts as relational management, and men sorely felt its absence. They interpreted their primary partner's failure to perform relational management as a lack of caring for them.

Further, the men reported upset at their partner's "nagging" to do household tasks. The men internalized that coupled with what they believed to be a failure to show gratitude for the work they did do as disappointment in them. This sense of themselves as a disappointment to their partner weighed heavily on them. They grew resentful, dissatisfied, and unhappy in their primary partnerships as a result. This chapter examines the theoretical framework of nagging and the ways that gendered power dynamics create nagging, as well as the economy of gratitude, both of which help make clear the phenomenon at hand.

© The Author(s) 2020
A. M. Walker, *Chasing Masculinity,*
https://doi.org/10.1007/978-3-030-49818-4_3

Men expressed sadness that their primary partners failed to show interest in them, and spoke of an awareness of their own "fragile" egos, which they believed needed frequent bolstering. Men in this study reported a belief that their primary partners function as "impossible to please." They also spoke of deep-seated insecurities, and the ways that their primary partnerships fed those insecurities. Further, the men believed that the design of marriage as an institution served to make them feel badly about themselves.

Women as Relational Managers

With regard to emotional intimacy within marriages, gender plays a role. Specifically, men tend to depend upon women to bear responsibility for the emotional intimacy within a relationship. In what *The Atlantic* calls "concept creep," popular culture often calls this "emotion work." However, the term "emotion work" actually refers to the work involved in managing your own emotions, regulating them, and engaging in self-talk to change them should your emotions prove inconvenient (Hochchild, 1983). Specifically, emotion work describes actions that enhance the well-being of other people and make them more comfortable (Hochchild, 1983) through managing your own emotional response. Thus, the actions most often referred to in popular culture as "emotion work" constitute a misuse of the term.

The actions referred to in popular culture when discourse evokes "emotion work" are really acts of what I call relational management. Within marriages and other intimate relationships, women bear the brunt of regulating the emotional life of both parties as U.S. cultural expectations demand it (Daniels, 1987). Women in heterosexual relationships often cope with both their own emotional life and that of their partner's. How? They inquire about his feelings; they monitor his moods and try to intuit what he fails to share; they enact practices aimed at relieving his stress, sadness, and frustration. In fact, women enter marriages groomed for this role due to their socialization and gendered expectations (Goleman, 1985). U.S. social expectations place the care for the smooth running of the household on women. Additionally, women feel responsible for apologizing after arguments, broaching relationship problems so they might be addressed, and even showing affection. However, men and women see relational management differently. Specifically, while women view it as "work," men often conceive of women's provision of relational management as just an expected part of a romantic relationship, and as an indicator of their partner's depth of feelings for them.

The requirement that women undertake relational management functions as an outgrowth of the U.S. cultural presentation of men and women as opposites of the same coin (England, 2010; Ridgeway, 2009; West & Zimmerman, 1987). These cultural ideas, which position women as emotional and men nearly absent emotion, not only shape norms around gendered behavior, but also contribute to cultural views of such behavior as "natural" (Ganong & Larson, 2011). In other words, we see stereotypical behavior by gender as "inherent" to that gender. You can see this in statements such as "women are emotional" and "men are not interested in feelings." But also in expectations that women nurture and that men receive that nurturing. Individuals internalize these cultural ideas and then reflect them in their behavior and experiences (Elliott & Umberson, 2008; West & Zimmerman, 1987).

U.S. society requires men to enact masculinity, which refers to the norms, ideologies, and practices within a culture that dictate what it means to be a man or not be a man (Levant, 2008). In Western culture, society socializes men to be "strong," defined as not expressing emotion. Under this framework we consider emotions a feminine expression, thus we expect men to remain stoic (Levant, 1997; Levant & Wimer, 2013; Mahalik et al., 2003; Pollack, 1998). Expectations of gender in U.S. culture require men to avoid showing their emotions, especially if those include sadness. American men especially experience socialization throughout the life course encouraging the belief that "real men" refrain from expressing emotions as this renders them weak (Pollack, 1998; Prentice & Carranza, 2002). Further, we provide no training to men and boys on how to manage their emotions. This lack of training (beyond "boys don't cry") leaves men without the know-how to manage their emotional lives well, making them dependent upon their romantic relationships as an outlet. When women continually perform the work of emotionally connecting with and providing emotional care to unreciprocating husbands, resentment and frustration grow.

As a result of these expectations of stoicism, men rely on women as an outlet for emotional expression and the provision of relational management. Divorced men tend to attach greater importance to having a partner, and report higher levels of loneliness, likely a result of their smaller support networks (Dykstra & Fokkema, 2007). Given the constant socialization in American society telling men to "buck up and be a man"—performed through shutting down their emotional expressions—it makes sense that they rely upon women as a safe space to express and unpack emotional responses. However, when men share their emotions with a woman, they risk having her laugh at them, shame them, or even invalidate their masculinity altogether (Brooks, 1995). Thus, society places men in a difficult position: they rely on women as their emotional outlet, but they risk their very sense of themselves as masculine each time they express vulnerability.

The men in this study relied upon their primary partners for relational management, and when they perceived its withholdment, they experienced that as a hurtful rejection. For these men, relational management functions both as their primary partner's responsibility, but also an expression of care. Thus, when they believe their primary partner to refrain from its provision, they grow resentful and unhappy with the relationship as a whole. Further, they begin to question what their primary partner's unwillingness to perform relational management says about them, both as a partner and a man. Due to gendered socialization of men that requires an absence of emotional expression, men function in a system where their emotional life depends upon their romantic partner. Thus, the loss of relational management in their primary partnerships proved detrimental for their sense of well-being.

"Show Interest in Me!"

Men described primary partnerships where they no longer felt valued, heard, or even seen. They believed their spouse to have lost complete interest in them as individuals. Holden (41, married) said, "For the most part, she is too enveloped in her own issues to notice a little sadness." Many men framed their wife's disinterest as an outcome of her own self-interest. Travis (43, married) explained:

> Mentally, there might be a degree of… depression(?) or at least melancholy, to which I respond by shutting down. I don't think my PP [primary partner] has ever noticed, though (she's somewhat self-absorbed)—at least she's never verbalized it. My wife has her own issues. That means she doesn't see or appreciate what I do, so [she] doesn't give me what I need.

It's impossible to know whether their primary partners' "own issues" refer to running the household, keeping a job outside the home, maintaining friendships, etc., or some other set of concerns entirely. The failure of their wives to perform high levels of relational management and indulge their need for attention provoked bitterness and resentment within the men.

Throughout these narratives existed a rather dim view of their primary partner's intentions, motivations, and attitudes. Many men saw their wives as simply "too busy" to meet their needs, which included offering praise, inquiring about their emotional well-being, adjusting to address their unhappiness, and giving them a great deal of attention. Without speaking to their primary partners, it's impossible to know whether the men's perceptions are valid. What matters is that the men themselves believe this to be their circumstances. Our belief that something is true functions as truth (Thomas & Thomas, 1928).

"Notice My Feelings"

Many men spoke of unvoiced sadness, unhappiness, or discontent. Holden expects his wife to "notice" his feelings, but he doesn't tell her about them. Again, this functions as an outgrowth of masculinity in the United States where the expectation of men is to keep their feelings to themselves. In fact, stoicism functions as a requirement for men claiming roles of power and performing masculinity (Sattel, 1976). Some men often engage in a "pattern of… controlling, distancing, and sometimes needy behaviors that harm relationships" as a result of relational deficits (Keith, 2017, p. 396). Flood and Donaldson refer to these relational deficits as mascupathy, "a pathology of masculinity caused by injurious male socialization, resulting in ruined lives and relationships" (Donaldson & Flood, 2014). Western society teaches boys to be men through silencing their own emotional expression (Keith, 2017). As a result, for many men, expressing their feelings simply isn't an option. "Men hide their feelings from loved ones to avoid appearing unmanly" (Keith, 2017, p. 398). Thus, Holden's expectation that his wife "notice" his sadness without his verbalizing it aligns with society's expectations of him. The narratives in this study suggest men believed they lacked the autonomy to simply voice their feelings; men believed that in order for their feelings to be voiced and addressed, their primary partner must notice them and inquire.

Correspondingly, his wife bears the responsibility for managing not only her own emotions, but also her partner's, so as to manage the well-being of the relationship, including broaching the topic of his demeanor of sadness. For example, Holden relies on his wife to help manage his emotional life without him prompting her to do so. While it's easy for us to scoff at these men's reactions and perceptions, it's important that we step back and consider their reports in context. These men function within a U.S. perspective that requires stoicism as an expectation of masculinity. They've been thoroughly socialized that "boys don't cry" and that expressing feelings is something only girls do. The only tools U.S. society bestowed on them with regard to their emotional lives is the mandate that they "suck it up" and "man up." What's that old saying? If all you have is a hammer, everything looks like a nail? When we examine romantic relationships through the lens of this training and socialization, the men's behaviors make more sense. These men genuinely felt that they couldn't simply approach their wives and voice their sadness. They believed they had to *wait* for her to approach them and inquire. Further, they internalized her failure to do so as a signal of her lack of care, concern, and interest in him. While in the United States we've empowered women with campaigns of "you go, girl" and encouraged them to "have it all," we've failed to socialize boys to grow into men equipped to function as equal partners—at least on an emotional level. We've also failed to expand definitions of masculinity and offer boys more options for ways of being, doing, and knowing themselves as men. Instead, we've continued to demand hegemonic masculinity from men, which includes the expectation that men ignore their own feelings at all costs. The natural outcome of this mandate is that he can *only* address his feelings with the assistance of his female romantic partner. Thus, these narratives illustrate one possible outcome of this paradigm. (Note: I'm not suggesting all men internalize the paradigm equally, nor that all men will/do/want to cheat.)

I cannot know whether the men's wives truly lacked interest in their emotional lives, or merely assumed the men were "fine" due to the men's own impression management. (Impression management, a term originated by Erving Goffman, refers to our attempts to influence how others see us/someone else/events through presenting a performance of what we believe is expected [Goffman, 1959]). It's impossible to know whether these men gave any clear indication of distress that their wives ignored. All I have are the men's perceptions. Whether their wives truly lacked interest in them or not, their perception served as reality. These men believe their wives lack interest in them, and thus operate as if that's the reality.

While the loss of satisfying, sensual sex proved difficult to endure (discussed further in Chapter 5), the men reported the loss of attention, praise, and validation most challenging. For these men, their spouses' interest in them, their day, their lives, and them as a sexual partner served to validate their masculinity. However, these relationships also helped them manage their emotional lives. Thus, men's experiences with affairs served to rectify the loss of validation, attention, praise, but most importantly, the loss of relational management, which men felt they needed to express and address their own feelings. In my previous study, most of the women pursued outside partnerships solely for their own sexual pleasure (Walker, 2018), but like a small group of women in that study with emotionally unsatisfying primary partnerships, these men sought them to outsource their emotional needs. Both men and women exercised outside partnerships as the Infidelity Workaround to avoid the pain and stigma of a divorce while getting their needs met by a more interested third party. The only difference between their experiences existed in the specific needs they sought to outsource due to the conditions of their primary partnerships.

Nagging: A Consequence of Gendered Notions of Relationships

Our commonsense understandings of heterosexual relationships remain heavily gendered. A common trope about marriage is that wives are never pleased. Presentations abound of men's belief that whatever they do is "never enough." A quick *Google* search bears this out as a plethora of returns show articles and websites decrying men's ability to please women. Anti-feminist writer, Suzanne Venker's book, *The Alpha Female's Guide to Men and Marriage: How Love Works* advises women to harness their "feminine" energy, evidenced by a wife not telling her husband "what do to" and being "soft" with him. Even *HuffPost* ran a feature called "Yes, Ladies, it IS your job to make your man happy," which admonished women to show more affection and verbalize more praise of their husbands. Television shows and films frequently depict husbands as afraid of upsetting their wives or as constantly falling short of pleasing them. In fact, in 1895, Cyrus Edison, a medical doctor, wrote and published an article called "Concerning Nagging Women," wherein he explained he was referring to the "woman who ceaselessly complains and scolds, and generally makes a nuisance of herself to every one [sic] who is cursed by being brought into contact with her" (Edson, 1895, p. 29). Thus, this concept of women as "naggers" exists as long-standing and embedded in gender stereotypes. In fact, in 2020, as part of *Oxford Dictionary*'s efforts to remove sexist language from their publication, they removed "nagging wife" as the example for the adjective "nagging."

Still this idea that wives nag persists. A 2014 *CBS* article about a study looking at nagging offered, "Ask any married guy on the planet and he'll tell you, as one man told *CBS2*, nagging is 'not pleasant.'" Nearly all of the media coverage of the study positioned nagging as the domain of wives. The study in question, a 2014 inquiry led by Rikke Lund, found that people who reported frequent demands and worries placed upon them by their spouses or children experienced a 50–100% higher risk of mortality when compared to those with peaceful lives (Lund, Christensen, Nilsson, Kriegbaum, & Rod, 2014). The researchers found that men "were especially vulnerable to frequent worries/demands from their partner." Further, they reported that demanding partners and children produce this effect. Demands from other people in men's lives failed to have this effect.

A possible reason for this positioning of wives as "nagging," "demanding," and "impossible to please" may stem from social expectations of gender. That is, the persistent cultural expectations that women perform the bulk of the housework and household management (Bianchi, Sayer, Milkie, & Robinson, 2012). As Dr. Karen Ruskin told *Healthline* in 2016, "women often take on the job of home management [and] men may label wives' repetitive requests as nagging" (Alexander, 2016). Diane Boxer found in 2002 that nagging tends to focus on the completion of household chores (Boxer, 2002). Boxer further explains that the need to nag arises from a lack of power. That is, if the person responsible for getting the chores done held more power, they wouldn't need to nag because the "nagee" would honor their requests at the first ask. The fact that the nagger lacks the power to provoke completion of requests upon first ask necessitates the act of nagging. Therefore, Boxer explains, this lack of power "appears to be the key to why it is that women are so frequently the naggers" (Boxer, 2002, p. 55). In fact, men may resist completing the chore upon first ask in an effort to "imagine he is doing it of his own free will" (Tannen, 1990, p. 31). Tannen explains that part of his resistance is that men don't want anyone "telling them what to do," "especially a woman" (Tannen, 1990, p. 31). Thus, nagging exists as a byproduct of gendered power dynamics within marriages.

This understanding proves useful to unpacking men's experiences. The men in this study function under the patriarchal system that teaches them to resist having anyone tell them what to do, especially when that someone is a woman. They bring that tendency into their marriages and romantic partnerships. The power dynamic where men fail to feel the need to respond to their primary partner's first request creates the conditions that lead to her nagging. The men then internalize the nagging as evidence of her unhappiness and disappointment in him. Yet, they continue to resist her first request for a task—nor do they look around and determine what needs to be done without being asked, a situation where the chore completion would, in fact, be of their own free will. While it may be easy to simply hold the men at fault, we must remember that the system oppresses all of us; it just looks different depending upon our particular statuses (hooks, 2004). Both these men and their primary partners function under this dynamic, and both suffer as a result.

The Economy of Gratitude

Another useful concept here is Hochschild's economy of gratitude, which refers to the central question of who is showing gratitude to whom and for what? (Hochchild, 1989, 2003). When one partner performs domestic tasks, they may experience that as a personal burden to themselves, but as a gift to their partner. In that mindset, if the laboring partner perceives a lack of gratitude from the non-laboring partner, feelings of dissatisfaction and inequity may ensure. The men in this study internalized the combination of their primary partner's nagging about domestic chores coupled with what the men perceived as their primary partner's failure to express gratitude for having completed the chores as evidence of their primary partner's disappointment in them. Perhaps their primary partners did fail to show gratitude for the completion of the tasks *because* the men only did so after being nagged. Perhaps their primary partners believed they expressed gratitude, but the men failed to internalize it as such. It's impossible for us to know the actual dynamics at play. What matters is that the men believe their primary partners failed to express gratitude for the domestic work they performed, and that their primary partners frequently nagged them to perform more chores— hence their perception that their primary partners are "impossible to please."

This concept coupled with the gendered nature of nagging and the importance of relational management further helps clarify the men's experience. Men rely on their primary partners for emotional expression and management. Men resist the first ask of their primary partners with regard to chores because of deeply ingrained gender and power dynamics, resulting in their primary partners nagging them. Men internalize that nagging as evidence that they disappoint their primary partners. Finally, when their primary partners fail to praise the men for doing the chores they had to nag them to do, the men experience further resentment, anger, hurt, and dissatisfaction. At no time do the men see the vicious cycle playing out in their household: they fail to do what their primary partners ask at first request, which necessitates nagging, which likely causes their primary partner to withhold praise, which results in the men feeling upset. The men experience this dynamic as upsetting, but also mysterious. They assume some failure of theirs as the root cause, but internalize that as a failure of character, manliness, and worthiness as a man.

"Marriage Trains Us to Feel Badly About Ourselves"

The men in this study described a sense of powerlessness within their primary partnerships, and described primary partners as impossible-to-please. These men experienced their primary partnerships as absent praise and validation. They perceived their primary partners as impossible to please, in part because of the constant requests (nagging). Patrick (33, married) explained, "Wife doesn't give a sh#t about my day, my work or my interests, even after I just spent the last 3 hours helping her with hers?? That's okay. My friend and I like to talk about our work to each other." When men spoke of helping their wives out, they described clear expectations that she return the gesture by bestowing attention and praise upon them. In fact, the men's narratives present the decision to "help out" as motivated by their expectation of quid pro quo from their wives, namely, attention, praise, and relational management. The men in the study felt that any chore or task they completed at home constituted "help" to their primary partner. In other words, these domestic tasks fell to the responsibility of their primary partner rather than themselves. Thus, their domestic labor served as a favor that should be repaid with praise and attention.

Men sought outside partners to provide praise, which resulted in a shift in their view of marriage as an institution. Riley (39, married) explained:

> The more someone else shows me I'm worth caring about, the more I start to dare to believe it. My internal dialogue has begun to change. I am appreciating things about myself again, not just finding fault in everything like a spouse trains us to do.

Notice the language Riley uses here. He claims that our spouses "train" us to feel badly about ourselves, to find fault within ourselves. This sense of primary partners as someone they continually failed to please and whose expectations they couldn't meet came up repeatedly. In many of the narratives, men position their wives as the director of the home, an uncompromising taskmaster, who constantly disapproves and whose expectations cannot be met. Men frequently described their wives as "nagging," constantly finding fault, and stingy with praise. These descriptions certainly call into question the marital dynamics in the United States. However, we cannot know the accuracy of these descriptions. We only know that these are the men's perceptions, which function as real to them. Without speaking to their primary partners, it's impossible to know whether these women truly incessantly nag the men or maintain impossible-to-reach standards. When asked to provide specific instances or specific comments their primary partners made as examples, nearly all of the men failed to deliver. Men waved that request off as though it lacked importance. And, for them, it doesn't. Their stated descriptions function as their reality of their primary partnerships. In their minds, their primary partners don't see them as capable, desirable, or pleasing. They've internalized the dynamics in those relationships as a condemnation of them *and* their masculinity. For the men in this study, that's what's real and true. This could correlate with the average age of men in this study (45.9), prime "midlife crisis" years. "As women become more assertive and men become more nurturing in later life, men become more vulnerable to psychological distress" (Keith, 2017, p. 405). In fact, when men reach midlife, they often "feel that there is something they need to prove" (Keith, 2017, p. 405). Thus, it's certainly possible that the men's perceptions of the dynamics of their primary partnership are in fact skewed, a result of their own distress about aging and fears that they are losing relevance.

This calls a few things into question. Is this a sample of men with especially critical wives? Are these wives a group of impossible-to-please folks? Without speaking to their wives, it's impossible to know with any certainty. However, I noticed an interesting pattern. Only three of the men offered examples of exchanges or stories of times where their wife nagged them, insulted them, or refused to be pleased by their contributions. By contrast, the women I spoke with who described unhappy or unhealthy marriages provided without prompting multiple detailed examples of their complaints. (Note: only a few women in my previous study claimed unhealthy marriages.) But those few women gave numerous concrete examples and stories without being asked. In this sample, most men didn't claim unhealthy or unhappy marriages. Most didn't even posit that their wives were bad people. They simply believed that the reality of marriage as an institution is that the wife nags, demands, and then refuses to recognize their husband's efforts, and can never be pleased. With only three exceptions, these men didn't see their marital dynamics as unusual or unhealthy, merely as typical. (Like the women with whom I spoke, the three men who described unhealthy or abusive dynamics provided multiple examples to illustrate.) Even with prompting, most men in this sample provided no concrete examples or stories to bolster their depictions of their wives. But their own sense of their primary partners as impossible-to-please, constantly disappointed, and continually nagging remained salient and real for them.

"Men's Egos Need Constant Pumping up"

Because men experienced their primary partnerships as spaces where they could never please their partners, soothing hurt feelings proved more important than society might imagine. Although U.S. social discourse often positions men's feelings as not terribly important, these men clearly understood that they were. As Ozzy (41, married) explained, "Men need their egos pumped up regularly. We are fragile creatures under all the bravado." Fragility wore throughout these narratives. Men consistently described hurt feelings, bruised egos, and an enormous need for attention and praise. These men's secret lives appeared to be ones where constant external validation is needed and even constructive criticism feels like an attack. Most of the men in this study expressed a similar sentiment to Riley's belief that a spouse—not just his, but any spouse—"trains you" to feel badly about yourself and to only see your flaws. This positions their wives as warden, and the men as prisoners, albeit willing prisoners. These narratives have implications for therapists attempting to address the fallout from the discovery of infidelity within a marriage.

Conclusion

The men in this study complained of wives who lost interest in them, their lives, their feelings, and them as sexual partners. Men regarded marriage as spaces where primary partners eventually stopped performing relational management, grew impossible to please, nagged constantly, and oversaw their household labor without offering praise. The economy of gratitude and the gendered nature of marital power dynamics that led to nagging come to bear here.

The men spoke of expectations that their primary partners ask about their emotional state rather than initiating a conversation about their sadness themselves. In fact, they believed they lacked the autonomy to voice their feelings without prompting and probing from their romantic partner.

Men in this study spoke of primary partnerships missing the level of validation, attention, and praise they deeply desired and expected. Further, men expressed discontent with their primary partner's failure to provide relational management, leaving the men to cope with their own emotions. They reported a desire for their primary partners to notice their feelings and probe about them, yet failed to voice their feelings to their primary without prompting.

The current common dynamic that places women as responsible for managing the household combined with the gendered power dynamics of romantic relationships provokes women's nagging. Men resist those requests, so that by the time they complete the chore in question, their primary partners likely withhold praise out of irritation. Men experience this dynamic as proof that they disappoint their partners, a belief that provokes much hurt and self-doubt. Men further believe their primary partners lack interest in hearing about their day, a slight they find particularly hurtful after they just "helped" their wife with a task. The men clearly see household labor as the work of their partners, thus any chore they complete becomes "help" to their wife. This framework positions their primary partner as "in charge" at home, yet men resent that being told what to do. This sets up a "you versus me" dynamic which is serving neither party. Given this cycle, it's certainly possible primary partners do indeed lack interest in the details of men's lives as a function of their frustration at being responsible for the household yet lacking the power to effect timely cooperation. Still, men fail to see the ways this sequence of interaction creates the conditions where they experience self-doubt, hurt feelings, and unmet needs.

References

Alexander, R. (Producer). (2016, March 17). *A nag a day keeps the doctor away*. Retrieved from https://www.healthline.com/health-news/nag-a-day-keeps-doctor-away#1.

Bianchi, S. M., Sayer, L. C., Milkie, M. A., & Robinson, J. P. (2012). Housework: Who did, does or will do it, and how much does it matter? *Social Forces, 91*(1), 55–63. https://doi.org/10.1093/sf/sos120.

Boxer, D. (2002). Nagging: The familial conflict arena. *Journal of Pragmatics, 34*(1), 49–61. https://doi.org/10.1016/S0378-2166(01)00022-4.

Brooks, G. R. (1995). *The Jossey-Bass social and behavioral science series. The centerfold syndrome: How men can overcome objectification and achieve intimacy with women*. San Francisco, CA: Jossey-Bass.

Daniels, A. K. (1987). Invisible work. *Social Problems, 34*(5), 403–415. https://doi.org/10.2307/800538.

Donaldson, C., & Flood, R. (2014). *Mascupathy: Understanding and healing the malaise of American manhood*. Grand Rapids, MI: Institute for the Prevention & Treatment of Mascupathy.

Dykstra, P. A., & Fokkema, T. (2007). Social and emotional loneliness among divorced and married men and women: Comparing the deficit and cognitive perspectives. *Basic and Applied Social Psychology, 29*(1), 1–12. https://doi.org/10.1080/01973530701330843.

Edson, C. (1895). Concerning nagging women. *The North American Review, 160*(458), 29–37.

Elliott, S., & Umberson, D. (2008). The performance of desire: Gender and sexual negotiation in long-term marriages. *Journal of Marriage and Family, 70*(2), 391–406. https://doi.org/10.1111/j.1741-3737.2008.00489.x.

England, P. (2010). The gender revolution: Uneven and stalled. *Gender & Society, 24,* 149–166. https://doi.org/10.1177/0891243210361475.

Ganong, K., & Larson, E. (2011). Intimacy and belonging: The association between sexual activity and depression among older adults. *Society and Mental Health, 1,* 153–172. https://doi.org/10.1177/2156869311431612.

Goffman, E. (1959). *The presentation of self in everyday life.* New York: Anchor.

Goleman, D. (1985). *Emotional intelligence.* New York: Bantam.

Hochchild, A. R. (1983). *The managed heart: Commercialization of human feeling.* Berkeley: University of California Press.

Hochchild, A. R. (1989). *The second shift: Working parents and the revolution at home.* New York, NY: Viking.

Hochchild, A. R. (2003). *The commercialization of intimate life: Notes from home and work.* Berkeley: University of California Press.

hooks, b. (2004). *Will to change: Men, masculinity, and love.* New York, NY: Washington Square Press.

Keith, T. (2017). *Masculinities in contemporary American culture.* New York: Routledge.

Levant, R. F. (1997). The masculinity crisis. *The Journal of Men's Studies, 5*(3), 221–231.

Levant, R. F. (2008). How do we understand masculinity? An editorial. *Psychology of Men & Masculinity, 9*(1), 1–4. https://doi.org/10.1037/1524-9220.9.1.1.

Levant, R. F., & Wimer, D. J. (2013). Masculinity constructs as protective buffers and risk factors for men's health. *American Journal of Men's Health, 8*(2), 110–120. https://doi.org/10.1177/1557988313494408.

Lund, R., Christensen, U., Nilsson, C. J., Kriegbaum, M., & Rod, N. H. (2014). Stressful social relations and mortality: A prospective cohort study. *Journal of Epidemiology and Community Health, 68,* 720–727.

Mahalik, J. R., Locke, B. D., Ludlow, L. H., Diemer, M. A., Scott, R. P. J., Gottfried, M., & Freitas, G. (2003). Development of the conformity to masculine norms inventory. *Psychology of Men & Masculinity, 4*(1), 3–25.https://doi.org/10.1037/1524-9220.4.1.3.

Pollack, W. S. (1998). Mourning, melancholia, and masculinity: Recognizing and treating depression in men. In W. S. Pollack & R. F. Levant (Eds.), *New psychotherapy for men* (pp. 147–166). Hoboken, NJ: Wiley.

Prentice, D. A., & Carranza, E. (2002). What women and men should be, shouldn't be, are allowed to be, and don't have to be: The contents of prescriptive gender stereotypes. *Psychology of Women Quarterly, 26,* 269–281.

Ridgeway, C. L. (2009). Framed before we know it: How gender shapes social relations. *Gender and Society, 23*(2), 145–160. https://doi.org/10.1177/089 1243208330313.

Sattel, J. W. (1976). The inexpressive male: Tragedy or sexual politics? *Social Problems, 26*(4), 469–477. https://doi.org/10.1525/sp.1976.23.4.03a 00090.

Tannen, D. (1990). *You just don't understand: Women and men in conversation.* New York: Morrow.

Thomas, W. I., & Thomas, D. S. (1928). *The child in America: Behavior problems and programs.* New York: Knopf.

Walker, A. M. (2018). *The secret life of the cheating wife: Power, pragmatism, and pleasure in women's infidelity.* Lanham, MD: Lexington Books.

West, C., & Zimmerman, D. H. (1987). Doing gender. *Gender and Society, 1*(2), 125–151.

4

"We Need a Witness to Our Lives": Outside Partners as Outsourced Relational Managers

Introduction

Ultimately, men reported that their primary partnerships failed to provide much-needed relational management, including praise and validation, which men felt they needed to bolster their sense of themselves as masculine. Outside partnerships served as a space where emotional needs could be met. Outside partners provided validation and attention, which helped soothe hurt feelings originating within the dynamics of their primary partnerships. The provision of relational management, validation, and praise proved wholly valuable and, more importantly, reaffirmed their masculinity. Ultimately, outside partners helped men's sense of their self-esteem, which lagged as a result of their perceptions of their primary partners' lack of interest in them. The men in this study internalized that perceived lack of interest as an indictment of their masculinity. Outside partnerships healed their self-esteem, which in turn improved their sense of themselves as masculine. For these men, outside partnerships served as a band-aid for the hurts and injuries—imagined or real—within their primary partnerships. Ultimately, men attempted to outsource their emotional needs to an interested third party as an Infidelity Workaround.

© The Author(s) 2020
A. M. Walker, *Chasing Masculinity*,
https://doi.org/10.1007/978-3-030-49818-4_4

Outsourcing Relational Management to Outside Partners

In response to their discontent within their primary partnerships, these men sought outside partners out of a need for relational management. Outside partners functioned as an Infidelity Workaround for the men in this study. That is, they avoided painful divorces while outsourcing their emotional needs. Outside partnerships provided help in terms of managing negative emotions and frustration regarding unmet expectations within their marriages. The stress-reducing capacity of outside partnerships helped men exercise more tolerance in their households. Sloan (36, married) explained:

> The outside relationship is like having my own secret oasis. When work or something else in my life gets really stressful, having that next meeting to look forward to makes the bad times easier to handle. When we're together the outside world melts away, and for however long we're together the focus is just on relaxing, having fun, and enjoying each other's company. Hard to quantify how precious that can be :-)

These narratives echoed those of the women in my previous book, who also used words like "oasis" and "vacation" to describe the stress-relieving effect of participation in outside partnerships. Beyond that, the men reported outside partnerships as spaces where they received emotional support. Ozzy (41, married) explained, "I get constant encouragement [from my outside partner]." This proved important to these men.

Outside partners served as a much-needed outlet to talk about their days, their frustrations, and their feelings. Years ago, someone related to me a story of the demise of one marriage and the creation of another. The friend told me of a couple, whose relationship began as an affair while the man was married to someone else. The man—we'll call him Jack—shared with his outside partner that he knew the exact moment his marriage ended. In his job as a police officer, Jack came upon a car accident where two teenage girls were trapped inside a burning vehicle. Although he tried everything, Jack couldn't free the girls from the car and had to stand listening to their agonized screams as they died. One girl begged him to shoot her and end her suffering, but Jack couldn't bring himself to do so. That event haunted him, so when Jack returned home that morning, he needed to talk about it with his wife, who refused to listen. Instead, she ignored him, walking away as he spoke, and left for work. Jack told his outside partner (who later became his second wife) "that was the moment my marriage ended." For Jack, his primary partner's unwillingness to help him manage his feelings around this incredibly traumatic moment functioned as a deal-breaker. In that moment, he felt so rejected and without support, he was done with the marriage. That experience opened the door for his affair, and eventual divorce and remarriage. He sought out an outside partner who listened and provided relational management, something he believed his first marriage lacked.

During the conversations in this study, I thought back to that story again and again. Granted, the men in this study aren't trying to share traumatic car accidents, but they did feel the need to share the details of their lives with someone. I'm reminded of a participant in *The Secret Life of the Cheating Wife*, Sophie, who said, "We need a witness to our lives. There's a billion people on the planet. I mean, what does any one life *really* mean?" (Walker, 2018). While it's tempting to dismiss these men's concerns as childish, trivial, and selfish, perhaps we do need someone to bear witness to our lives. Jack needed his wife's help unpacking, making sense of, and living with what he'd witnessed. His wife refused. His friend listened, and they became lovers and eventually spouses. Had Jack's wife simply listened to him—if not that morning, then later that evening—might they have remained married? Clearly, the men in this study don't want to leave their primary partnerships, and none reported witnessing anything horrifying they needed to share. However, the importance of a partner's willingness to listen to us cannot be overstated.

"Emotional Intimacy" or Friendship?

Outside partners listened to them, but they also lavished attention on the men. Men's outside partnerships helped fill the void left behind in marriages where they believed their primary partner lost interest in them both as a person and a lover. Thus, within their outside partnerships, what men called "emotional intimacy" ranked high on their "musts" list. Riley (39, married) said:

> I chose *Ashley Madison* because it needed to be more than just sex. It was human touch and intimacy that was the most needed. It had to be emotional as well. My outside relationship provides the emotional and physical connection that has been absent in my marriage.

Notice his emphasis on the importance of the emotional nature of the affair. This idea came up again and again in these narratives. This stands in contrast to most of the women's reports in my previous study on women's infidelity, which stated they sought sexual gratification, not emotional connection. However, the vast majority of women in that study reported a solid emotional connection with their primary partner. Thus, outsourcing the emotionality of their relationship proved unnecessary. Only seven of those women reported a lack of emotional intimacy in their primary partnerships. Like the men in this study, those seven women also outsourced the emotional aspect of their marriage.

But more importantly, men truly believed they got emotional intimacy from affairs. Yet the narratives clearly describe outside partners who supply praise, attention, and validation. They described dynamics that served to bolster men's sense of themselves as men and confirmed their masculinity. However, when a female partner evoked those feelings, these men *experienced* that as emotional intimacy.

If you read my previous book detailing women's participation in outside partnerships, while reading this book you may be asking yourself, "If the women only wanted sex and no emotional intimacy, but the men are seeking emotional intimacy and think they're getting it… how can both of these things be true at once?" The key to understanding these narratives side-by-side lies in understanding that these men framed the provision of emotional support as "intimacy," while the women I interviewed would deem these behaviors as simple "friendship," to which they weren't opposed. We also have to consider that the women in my previous study experienced U.S. socialization, which directs women to act with caring and concern for others, especially men. These women were showing kindness to the men, who internalized the resulting rise in their self-esteem as "emotional intimacy." The women I spoke with eschewed emotional intimacy with their outside partners— at least, beyond friendship and trust. They avoided men who sought emotional affairs. Yet this group of men claims emotional intimacy as the benefit of their outside partnerships. The realization that these men label as "emotional intimacy" women's provision of praise, caring, attention, and inquiries as to the quality of their day or how they feel exists as a key piece to understanding the phenomenon of inquiry here, especially as it juxtaposes to the experiences of women on *Ashley Madison*. The women in my previous study labeled that "friendship," not "intimacy." For the women in my previous study, "emotional intimacy" stood for feelings of "love," which they believed would threaten their primary partnerships, and thus couldn't be tolerated within an outside partnership. (In fact, they often couched it as "avoiding emotion," but that existed as a euphemism for "love" [Walker, 2018].) However, the women perceived friendship and trust as safe levels of emotional connection.

Additionally, the women admitted to telling their outside partners what they wanted to hear with regard to monogamy in affairs, and then doing as they pleased. Women reported that men on *Ashley Madison* wanted to find a partner who would see only them and no one else (this claim is backed up by men's narratives as well), but women often maintained multiple outside partnerships concurrently and simply withheld that information, or outright lied and told men they were "the only one." Given these understandings, it seems likely that between men's framing and women's tendency to say what men want to hear that both parties are accurately reporting their experiences. Yet men seem to place a high value on what they think is an "emotional connection," while women perceive this as just providing friendship to their outside partners.

Many men used the term "emotional intimacy" to describe a range of behaviors. For example, talking to their outside partner proved important to these men. Barry (37, married) explained, "When I started my outside relationship, I was not communicating with my [wife] and needed someone to talk to." Many men in this study talked explicitly about the value of being able to talk to their outside partner. When asked what they talked about, the conversations tended to fall into what friends talk about. Again, the women in my previous study didn't consider these friendship connections to be "emotional intimacy." Yet the men did. This represents a critical site of difference in men's and women's interpretations of their experiences. For the women I spoke with, talking with outside partners about your day and being supportive about their endeavors constituted friendship. Yet the men experienced that as "emotional intimacy." The difference in how they see this could lie in the differences in men's and women's friendship dynamics. For men, same-sex friendships require a performance of masculinity, which includes stoicism and self-reliance (Migliaccio, 2010). Thus, they may not disclose their feelings, hopes, dreams, and needs to same-sex friends given that male friendships tend to be less intimate and supportive than female friendships (Bank & Hansford, 2000). Thus, the difference in men's and women's understandings of the outside partnership dynamics may lie in the difference in their experiences of same-sex friendships, specifically expected level of disclosure, caring, and vulnerability.

Further, when we examine the meanings of "friendship" and "emotional intimacy" things get murky. Among scholars, emotional intimacy refers to a "perception of closeness to another that allows sharing of personal feelings, accompanied by expectations of understanding, affirmation, and demonstrations of caring" (Sinclair & Dowdy, 2005, p. 193). We define friendship "as a close, mutual, dyadic relationship" (Erdley & Day, 2017, p. 3). Thus, one might expect emotional intimacy within a friendship, which the women concede existed within their outside partnerships. Perhaps the men of this inquiry defaulted to "emotional intimacy" rather than "friendship" due to the nature of their same-sex friendships (i.e., absent intimate disclosure) discussed above. Because their friendships with their outside partners featured emotional disclosure and a level of openness possibly missing from their same-sex friendships, the term "friendship" likely felt an inadequate description of these connections. Whereas because women's friendships tend to include emotional disclosure and openness, they defaulted to the term "friendship."

One man in particular described a process of choosing outside partners based on existing friendship. Simon (39, married) described his history: "[My outside partnerships] were all long-term affairs that lasted months to years and consisted of much more than just physical intimate encounters." However, Simon explained that his participation in outside partnerships "developed over time out of friendship." He categorized those connections as "friendships" because the relationship "had meaning and substance." His participation then evolved into purely sexual one-time events. He later settled into his current outside partnership, a woman he found on *Ashley Madison*. That outside partnership taught him something about himself. He explained, "I am left with the understanding that it is not something sexual I am missing." Simon believed he sought both "passion and excitement" and "emotions and a connection" in his outside partnerships. (The search for passion and excitement and its meaning is discussed further in Chapter 6). However, it's important to note that Simon explained that at present he hasn't "been in a long-term relationship in 5 years," thus his current outside partnerships exist as temporary and short-term. While he made clear the value of the sexual activity within them, he also clearly saw these relationships as "emotionally intimate." Simon's experience proves important for unpacking men's experiences. Simon currently participates in only short-term outside partnerships, yet also sees these pairings as "emotionally intimate," a state of interaction we tend to see as existing within longer-term associations.

While these outside partnerships included sex, these men made clear their desire for "something more." Scott (40, married) explained:

> If all they wanted to do was bang and leave, that would be ok[ay], but I'd prefer a bit more. At best, my ideal OP would want to spend a bit of time playing, go a couple rounds between the sheets, even chit chat and drink wine together, just idling touching and such.

The men sought an emotional intimacy and connection with a sexual partner. Even the sex in their outside partnerships functioned to fill an emotional need, specifically their need to see themselves as masculine (i.e., the "Girlfriend Experience," discussed in Chapter 6).

The men valued having an emotional connection with a woman. Considering their perception of events proves important here. Barry (37, married) explained, "It started out innocent, as all relationships do, and she filled an emotional void I had in my life. Then over time we [became sexually involved]." Interesting that though Barry created a profile, logged on, vetted partners, and found an outside partner for an

extramarital affair, he believes "it started off innocent." Although clear
to the reader that logging on and finding an outside partner is not innocent at all, Barry's perception differed greatly. Not only does he see his
own outside partnership as beginning "innocently," he's convinced that
"all relationships" "start out as innocent." Unpacking this framing of his
entry into participation in outside partnerships as "innocent" helps us
better understand men's framing of women's provision of care, concern,
and friendship as "emotional intimacy." Previous research determined
that two-thirds of men on *Ashley Madison* had no intention of meeting a
partner face-to-face; rather, they used the site to explore the possibility of
an affair and to test their own desirability (Wolfe, 2011). Thus, Barry's
statement may reflect his original motivation, which functioned to test
the waters, or perhaps see if anyone might find him desirable. Perhaps
the connection formed during that exploration proved too tempting to
resist.

Men spoke of the need for this "emotional connection" to be in
place prior to their development of real sexual interest in an outside
partner. This echoed the small minority of seven women who sought
to outsource the emotional aspect of their marriages in my last study;
but stands in complete contrast to the bulk of women I spoke with
who often developed friendships with men *after* establishing a satisfying sexual relationship (Walker, 2018). Again, those women sought
to outsource the physical nature of their primary partnerships. Thus,
different priorities motivated their participation. These men spoke of
creating an "emotional bond" with an outside partner that led to sex.
Yes, they went to *Ashley Madison* to find this friendship and bond, so
sex was always on the table. They didn't slip and fall into an affair.
But that emotional support and validation gained from the under-
lying friendship superseded everything else in importance and preceded
everything physical. This challenges commonsense narratives of men's
sexuality and gendered sexuality. We tend to position men as uncaring
about emotional connections in sexual relationships and women as prioritizing them. The narratives of the men in this study and the women
in my previous book demonstrate that both groups valued emotional
connection. The bulk of the women had that at home with primary partners, and thus sought to outsource the physical. Yet both the women and

men whose primary partnerships lacked emotional intimacy sought to outsource the emotional connections they valued within sexual outside partnerships.

Some men even referenced "love" between their outside partner and themselves. Gus (62, married) said, "We tell each other we love each other (and I certainly love her…and I do believe she still loves me)." The sentiment of love was nearly absent in women's narratives, but ten men (roughly 22% of the sample) evoked the word with regard to their outside partnerships. Among the group of women in my previous study seeking to outsource only the sexual aspect of their primary partnerships, three (6.5%) reported miscalculating and experiencing "love" or something close to it (Walker, 2018). Among the seven women (roughly 15% of that sample) also seeking to outsource the emotional aspect of their primary partnerships, only two spoke of "love" for their outside partners (roughly 4% of the sample) (Walker, 2018).

Men demonstrated internalization of the U.S. cultural narrative regarding men's motivation to cheat and men's lack of emotionality. Thus, many men expressed a belief that *their* need for emotional connection (or emotional intimacy) made them unique. Simon (39, married) explained:

> I do feel like I am somewhat different from other men in that I do truly feel emotions and a connection in these interactions. I have a hard time splitting the difference between sex and "love." My friends who are girls always laugh and say I'm such a woman because I experience such deep emotion and connections and have a more traditional "feminine" approach to relationships in their eyes.

Simon cultivated friendships with women with whom he could confide his feelings and needs. To reconcile his expression of these needs with the dominant U.S. narrative about men, his friends labeled him "feminine." There also existed among the men an awareness of the judgment people had about infidelity. Riley (39, married) added:

> For anyone who thinks these outside relationships are just about sex, I just laugh and laugh and laugh. They have no idea, and their credibility to judge is a joke. Actual sex and orgasms are definitely more tangible parts

of these relationships, but also definitely in the minority of improvements the outside relationships bring.

Although sex functioned as a part of these outside partnerships, men's sense of an emotional intimacy served as the most critical. For men who perceived their marriages as lacking attention, validation, and praise, finding it in an outside partner proved critical. Men framed these friendly connections as emotional intimacy.

Men in this study reported placing a high value on the emotional support and validation gained from their outside partnerships. Men spoke of a loss of connection within their marriages, and described the ways their outside partners helped to fill those gaps. Social expectations of women posit that their affairs exist as an effort to seek out emotional connection and validation, while men's focus on sexual fulfillment. However, my previous study of women's infidelity found that most of those women clearly explained their motivations as sexual pleasure and orgasms (Walker, 2018). In fact, they purposefully vetted partners for an absence of emotional connection beyond trust and friendship, and preferenced partners with sexual compatibility and acumen. By contrast, these men sought emotional connections and valued emotional intimacy above sexual pleasure. The men in this study challenge common-sense understandings of infidelity and gender. Like the women in my previous study whose primary partnerships lacked emotional intimacy, men sought to outsource that aspect to an interested third party as an Infidelity Workaround.

Outside Partners Boost Men's Egos

Men reported experiencing an ego boost as a result of their participation in outside partnerships. For many men, this spilled over into their work life. Greg (53, married) said, "I am in a business development role and you need to have an air of confidence/competence to be good at what you do. OPs give me that." Men frequently reported that others noticed their enhanced self-confidence as well. Travis (43, married) explained:

The attention I get from my OP boosts my self-confidence and sense of self-worth (I ignore the fact I'm morally devoid in some people's eyes) and I think that reflects in both home and work. People at work have noticed a positive difference in my demeanor. I admit I do feel more confident, generally, with my OP around, and a little more flirtatious with other women, too.

Travis believed that the reassurance gained from his outside partnerships spilled over into his work and his social life. He wasn't alone. Sloan (36, married) explained:

Being desired and feeling attractive again has also boosted my self-esteem and improved my mood. It also gives me more energy. I definitely have more of a bounce in my step because of my outside relationship.

He believed the ego boost from his outside partnership touched every-thing in his life. Matteo (44, married) said, "I walk differently. I stand differently. I tolerate things differently. I'm calmer and I have WAY more patience. Friends and family have commented on my new demeanor." These men realized their very sense of self remained wrapped up in their sexual lives and the sense of masculinity gained. Thus, what happened in bed impacted their behavior in other spaces, i.e., work, social life.

Outside partnerships offered validation, but no ceiling existed as the amount needed. Matteo (40, married) added, "My personal masculinity is fed and elevated exponentially through the complexities of the rela-tionship. This is by far one of the most amazing transformations I have experienced." These men realized their sense of masculinity as tied up with the women in their lives. How their partners regarded them absolutely colored their self-esteem. Many men spoke of experiencing a turnaround in terms of self-esteem and feeling "like a man" as a result of these relationships. Ozzy (41, married) said:

She makes me feel attractive and virile. I get excitement in my life. The relationship with her makes me confident as a man, which relaxes me. I don't feel the need to prove things to people since I know I walk with a quiet confidence. I get someone who actively admires me. I get someone who is interested in the topics I'm interested in.

The men made clear that knowing they deliver in the bedroom changed how they interacted with the world. Having a partner praise and adore them provided confidence and removed the need to "prove" themselves to the outside world.

Finally, the men reported the healing power of the emotional connection and intimacy with their outside partners. Donald (61, married) described his experience: "I feel an outside partnership enhances my life in some way because it's important to me to feel appreciated, to feel loved, and to feel alive." Feeling appreciated—as evidenced through praise—came up repeatedly in these narratives. Men reported a need for a lot of praise in order to feel loved, worthy, and masculine. For these men, outside partnerships functioned as spaces where years of perceived neglect, rejection, and frustration melted away. Appealing to a man's ego clearly falls under the men's expectation of relational management. The men in this study valued partners who provided relational management, and they interpreted its provision as care and intimacy. The men's narratives here echo previous work showing that men's sense of failure in their ability to enact the norms of hegemonic masculinity led them to purchase sex in an effort to "feel like a man again" (Shumka, Strega, & Hallgrimsdottir, 2017). While the men in this study didn't purchase sex, they did participate in outside partnerships as an act of compensatory masculinity to regain their own sense of themselves as a masculine being. Thus, this Infidelity Workaround served both to outsource the emotional aspect of their primary partnerships and to boost their own sense of masculinity.

The provision of validation within their outside partnerships proved a salve for the hurt of their primary partnerships. Patrick (33, married) explained, "When I didn't have an OP [outside partner], and my wife was the only source of female companionship, I was more bothered by her distance and lack of connection and care for me." Outside partners performed relational management for these men. Byron (57, married) explained, "My OP does provide another sounding board for various issues or dilemmas that have come up and I have provided a sympathetic ear for her problems." Getting the attention they craved helped lessen the hurt and upset silently directed at their wives. Patrick (33, married) added, "At the daily level, I've been less bothered, and more at peace around my spouse. What I mean is, if she is naggy, distant, or dismissive, it doesn't bother me as much." Men spoke of an approach that permitted them to let go of their distress with their wives, to forgive the slights they endured. Men clearly saw the maintenance of their emotional lives as the responsibility of their wives. They perceived their outside partner as an outside contractor who took on the overflow work their wife could no longer handle alongside her other duties.

Men believed that their improved self-care improved their abilities in their primary relationships. Riley (39, married) added,

> Physically, it has been much better for my health. It has given me a reason to care about taking care of myself again. I've improved my hygiene habits. I am making better food choices and am not relying on self-medication with food to plug the emotional gaps I had. I am more active, getting more exercise, out and about in society more, less isolated.

It's not hard to imagine that when a person engages in better self-care (e.g., exercise, better diet), they are more equipped to handle life's little stressors. Sadly, primary partnerships failed to motivate men in this fashion.

Conclusion

Outside partners offered the emotional support, attention, interest, and validation these men believed their wives had stopped providing. The provision of this proved significant in their lives and enabled them to enact a better self in their "real lives." The emotional support and validation provided by their outside partners acted as a salve for hurt feelings, hurt egos, and damaged self-esteem. For these men, outside partners functioned as outsourced laborers who performed the relational management they desperately needed and that their wives failed to perform.

The men reported emotional intimacy as a prized facet of their outside relationships. However, it's important to note that what men call "emotional intimacy" here are behaviors the women in my previous study deemed "friendship" (and those women stated a desire to avoid "emotional intimacy" with their outside partners); however, the women used "emotional intimacy" as a euphemism for "love" (Walker, 2018). Men's framing of friendship as "emotional intimacy" likely stems from the differences in same-sex friendship dynamics, specifically that men's friendships often lack the self-disclosure and openness of those of women.

The difference in my findings and those of previous research may be due to a host of factors, for example, the fact that this sample is comprised of men who purposefully logged on and vetted partners rather than organically falling into affairs. The sense of confidentiality granted by the methodology (i.e., online recruitment and collection) may also be a factor. Also, the qualitative nature of this dataset may play a role. Men initially responded that they cheated for sex. Had they responded only to a survey question, they may have reported sex as their primary motivation. However, our conversations revealed other motivations as more salient.

In fact, within these narratives describing the difficulty of going without satisfying sex, men's larger concerns were the loss of "emotional intimacy," specifically, they complained that their wives no longer paid as much attention to them, failed to adequately praise and validate them. That loss proved much more upsetting. Men talked about the lack of validation in their marriages, and how devastating that loss was. However, the decision to seek and enter outside partnerships was not made lightly. The men in this study desired to remain in their primary partnerships for the foreseeable future. Prior to participation in outside partnerships, the men lacked confidence that doing so was actually possible. Many felt at the end of their capacity to endure when they turned to the activity of seeking an outside partner.

Like the women in my previous study, men participated in outside partnerships as an Infidelity Workaround. Specifically, they hoped to avoid the painful and costly measure of divorce by outsourcing the aspects of their primary partnerships that failed to meet their needs.

In my previous study, the bulk of the women interviewed lacked sexual satisfaction in primary partnerships. Thus, they outsourced that aspect. However, the seven women lacking an emotional connection in their primary partnerships outsourced that aspect, just as the men in this study attempt.

References

Bank, B. J., & Hansford, S. L. (2000). Gender and friendship: Why are men's best same-sex friendships less intimate and supportive? *Personal Relationships, 7*(1), 63–78. https://doi.org/10.1111/j.1475-6811.2000.tb00004.x.

Erdley, C. A., & Day, H. J. (2017). Friendship in childhood and adolescence. In M. Hojjat, A. Moyer, & A. M. Halpin (Eds.), *The psychology of friendship.* New York, NY: Oxford.

Migliaccio, T. (2010). Men's friendships: Performances of masculinity. *The Journal of Men's Studies, 17*(3), 226–241. https://doi.org/10.3149/jms.170 3.226.

Shumka, L., Strega, S., & Hallgrimsdottir, H. K. (2017). "I wanted to feel like a man again": Hegemonic masculinity in relation to the purchase of street-level sex. *Frontiers in Sociology, 2*(15). https://doi.org/10.3389/fsoc. 2017.00015.

Sinclair, V. G., & Dowdy, S. (2005). Development and validation of the emotional intimacy scale. *Journal of Nursing Measurement, 13*(3), 193–206. https://doi.org/10.1891/jnum.13.3.193.

Walker, A. M. (2018). *The secret life of the cheating wife: Power, pragmatism, and pleasure in women's infidelity.* Lanham, MD: Lexington Books.

Wolfe, L. (2011). The oral sex void: When there's not enough at home. *Electronic Journal of Human Sexuality, 14.*

5

"If I Was a Good Enough Man, She'd Be Jumping on Top of Me, Right?": Marital Beds Breed Self-Doubt

Introduction

Men reported lengthy past hurts and resentments within their primary partnerships. Specifically, they believed their primary partners lacked interest in them both as a sexual partner and as an individual. For these men, the dynamics of the marital bed served to sow self-doubt. They experienced this perceived lack of interest on the part of their primary partner as rejection. Men internalized this rejection as proof of their own lacking. They believed that their primary partners' lack of interest in them signaled some deficit within themselves. The shame of being such a disappointment ate at them over time. Taking on an outside partner helped the men reframe the dynamics of their primary partnerships. In other words, outside partners functioned as evidence that the problem must not be with them. The men believed that their participation in outside partnerships made them better able to act in healthy ways within their primary partnerships. Thus, the men believed that outsourcing their emotional needs in sexual outside partnerships benefitted both their primary partners as well as themselves.

© The Author(s) 2020
A. M. Walker, *Chasing Masculinity*,
https://doi.org/10.1007/978-3-030-49818-4_5

Scripts and Gendered Sexuality

The expectations of gender exist within U.S. sexual scripts, a concept recognized by social scientists. The research of Simon and Gagnon (1984, 2003) shows that our social behavior is socially scripted, including our sexual behavior (Simon & Gagnon, 1984, 2003). What do I mean by socially scripted? I mean that our interactions with others socialize us to internalize and self-police our own behavior through "scripts," which are frameworks we construct to make sense of our experiences, our own behavior, the behavior of other people, and the social expectations of behavior. Who is teaching us these scripts? Our parents, our peers, the media. We learn these expectations through both our own observation and internalizing of similar situations. We experience romantic and sexual scripts as particularly salient because they shape and inform our beliefs, thoughts, and actions (Alksnis, Desmarasis, & Woods, 1996; Paik & Woodley, 2005; Rose & Frieze, 1993; Simon & Gagnon, 1984). Scripts become guides showing us how to respond and react to situations.

The scripts exist all around us, so pervasive and ubiquitous that we rarely even notice them. What we write off as "inherent" and "biological" and "natural" is often socialization through these scripts. With regard to sexual behavior, these highly gendered scripts command one set of behaviors for men and another set for women. Sexual scripts for men grant sexual freedom, while women's sexual scripts dictate the primacy of love over sex, and further demand chaste behavior and a general disinterest in sex outside of a monogamous relationship. In turn, these accepted ideas about how men and women *should* behave become interwoven into our beliefs about how they *do* behave. We assume that other people's behavior reflects the expectations of these scripts. We often either curtail our own behavior to match those expectations, or we conceal that behavior which doesn't correspond. Men's sexual scripts demand sexual prowess as proof of manhood.

Marital Bed Breeds Self-Doubt

The men in this study described intense attunement to their sexual partner's responses and a propensity to internalize every lack of response as criticism of their performance and worth as a sexual partner. Thus, if they perceived their primary partner as disinterested in sexual activity—or lacking interest in prolonged sexual encounters—they interpreted that as an indictment of themselves. As a result, the marital bed functioned as a site fraught with opportunities for hurt feelings, wounded egos, and self-recrimination.

For the men in this study, the dynamics of their marital sex lives served as opportunities for perceived threats to their masculinity. They frequently felt inadequate and inferior in intimate situations with their wives. This deficiency caused them to question themselves. Patrick (33, married) said:

> This happened so fast in the marriage (recognizable in the first month) that it initially made me believe that it was my fault. If I was a good enough man, if I was sexy enough, if I had enough money and bought her nice things, romanced her with affection and attention... she'd be jumping on top of me, right?

This idea of following the sexual script—a prescription of behavior guaranteed to yield sex—only to have their wives ignore their efforts proved common in this study. The failure of their wives' behavior to conform to the expected response to their gendered sexual scripts deeply impacted men. Rather than question the validity of the social narrative surrounding gendered behavior, they assumed the fault rested within themselves. There lies the power of the gendered sexual scripts: if they fail to produce the desired result, people have so internalized these messages they still believe the fault belongs to them and rarely question the system itself. It encourages feelings of inadequacy. Patrick (33, married) explained:

I used to just wonder, ponder, "what did I do wrong this time?" when she clearly was bored out of her mind during lovemaking. It used to haunt me. I'd rebound, restudy, make a date night, buy her roses, send her off with her friends for a weekend, study how to be a better lover, ask her how I could be better, spend more time at home... I wasted so much time.

Here we see men following the social script around "love as consumption." For these men, the social script clearly mandated purchasing as a means of showing love. Heterosexual scripts provided by media encourage men to "assert their power in the courting ritual by buying gifts" and other behaviors (Kim et al., 2007, p. 148). Media presentations of relationships mold our romantic imaginations and shape our understandings of meanings and expectations within romantic relationships (C. Bachen & Illouz, 1995; C. M. Bachen & Illouz, 1996). Advertisements featuring men purchasing gifts for their wives abound. Car and jewelry commercials especially exercise this trope. Television shows and films often depict men purchasing gifts, and frequently as a means to apologize or get back into her good graces (e.g., *The Sopranos, Dexter, The Big Bang Theory*). There are even real-life examples. The now infamous story of George and Gracie Burns serves as an instance. George related an incident in his autobiography claiming that he'd cheated with a gorgeous starlet and to make it up to his wife, he gave her a silver centerpiece and a $10,000 diamond ring. He claimed that years later Gracie told a friend she wished he'd cheat again because she could use a new centerpiece. The script of gifts equal apology remains strong.

When men followed these scripts, they were supposed to be rewarded. Yet the social script failed Patrick. He studied and performed masculinity as prescribed, and yet his marriage did not yield the affection, desire, and sexual frequency he anticipated. This reality left him with two choices: either the script is faulty, or his masculinity is. Patrick strove to enact his ideal of masculinity, which pop cultural presentations have likely shaped. For him, this failure was about not being "man enough." Blaming themselves and internalizing the situation as a reflection of themselves as men served as the default. Patrick (33, married) added, "I was convinced I was just a horrible lover, unattractive, didn't make enough money, and probably had a substandard penis. I now realize she just doesn't find enjoyment in it or [find] me physically attractive." These experiences translated to self-doubt about prowess, penis size, and physical attractiveness, but also traits outside of the bedroom.

For most of the men in this study, their marital sex lives continually legitimized their concerns regarding their masculinity. Matteo (44, married) elaborated, "My wife to this day has not experienced an orgasm." Men whose wives had never experienced orgasm suspected their own lack of prowess as the reason. Given that the current conception of masculinity in the United States includes sexual prowess, these men internalized their wives' lack of orgasm as a failure of their own manhood. In their minds, they function as the provider of orgasms, and within their marital bed orgasms remain absent. Thus, the responsibility lies with them (More on this in Chapter 8).

Men described their primary partnerships as spaces where their sexual expression was shut down, ignored, not valued. Mitch (59, married) said, "I am very romantic; like to touch and cuddle and kiss. Wife is very different." Many men spoke of sexual needs that included a preference for romance, connection, sensuality, and intimacy. Again, this challenges U.S. conceptions of men's sexual desires and motivations. In the United States, we tend to believe men not only don't require romance, they're disinterested in it. The demands of masculinity position men as always ready for sex without the need of any aid and disinterested in mushy displays and gestures, only participating in them for the benefit of their female partner. The sex lives the men described with their spouses existed absent those things, and they study spoke of a deep need for that missing romance, sensuality, intimacy, and connection. Their narratives challenge the current commonsense understandings of gender that position men and women as opposites, and pose women as "emotional" and men as "lacking emotion."

The men in this inquiry spoke at length about their disappointment with the impersonal nature of the sexual encounters in their primary partnerships. They desired to feel wanted and to engage in sensual sexual contact. Mitch painted a vivid scene of a typical encounter in his marriage.

We have sex once or twice a week. "Perfunctory" is the best word I can think of to describe it. Most of the time her back is to me. She doesn't touch my genitals with her hands and won't allow me to touch hers. Oral sex of any kind is absolutely forbidden. She will not kiss me. I'm always the one who initiates it, and she has her eyes closed the whole time. Never smiles. Rarely makes any sound. With her back to me she moves her clitoris back and forth on my penis until she's ready, then rolls to her back and takes me on top, allowing me to enter her. We have vaginal intercourse for just a short time until she has an orgasm and I do too, after her.

This certainly doesn't read as descriptive of a loving, passionate encounter. Aside from the wife's orgasm, this description wasn't uncommon among these men. While reading this, it's easy to imagine our own response to such a dynamic: we'd be left wanting. So were these men.

Our primary partners stand as the person who loves us the most, our confidant, and our other half. If we've legally bound ourselves, this person stood in front of witnesses and vowed to love us above all others. Thus, when the sexual dynamics within the relationship function in the manner described, hurt feelings result. Our cultural tendency is to dismiss men's motivations for infidelity with statements like "men are dogs" and "men are so stupid they'll throw away a good woman for anyone willing to spread their legs," but these men's narratives describe real hurt and feelings of rejection. Men described sexual dynamics lacking connection and caring going back years and decades. We can surely put ourselves in these men's place and imagine our own hurt and upset. Thus, we can certainly understand what these men are going through. We, too, want our partners to want us.

Further, some researchers have posited that as a historically gendered and patriarchal institution, marriage itself remains built on men's "privilege and entitlement to women's labor, sexuality, and emotions" (Lorber, 2005, p. 159). In other words, men expect women to provide sexual access and emotional expression, including expressing desire. In fact, sex persists as a "signifier of love and marital bliss" (Elliott & Umberson, 2008, p. 394). In order to maintain that, the expectation remains that women perform the labor required to keep intimate relation-ships going, including the sexual aspect (Duncombe & Marsden, 1993; Hockey, Meah, & Robinson, 2012; Lodge & Umberson, 2012). Women remain culturally responsible for relationship management, including maintaining a satisfying sex life, within heterosexual relationships. This includes the performance of sexual desire and managing our own feelings about sex as well as our partners (Elliott & Umberson, 2008), something for which both partners feel responsible. We do this to "reduce marital conflict, enhance intimacy, help a spouse feel better about himself or herself, or all three" (Elliott & Umberson, 2008, p. 404). Further, Gabb (2019) found that relationship work (her term for the work required to maintain an ongoing sexual life within long-term partnerships) is required in heterosexual partnerships in order to "manage differences in sexual desire through 'accommodation' and 'compromise'" (Gabb, 2019). Thus, in these partnerships, men clearly feel that while they are performing desire, managing their own feelings about the sexual dynamics, and doing relationship work, their primary partners fail to do their part. Research shows that heterosexual men tend to struggle with discrepancies in sexual desire within their long-term intimate partner-ships (Gabb, 2019). Thus, the feelings and responses reported by the men in this study bear out previous research on long-term heterosexual pairings. While it may be tempting to write off these men's concerns, they represent the feelings of many in these situations.

While sharing their narratives, many men came to the realization that they harbored bitterness and resentment toward their wives as a result of the state of sexual contact between them. Mitch realized:

When I read what I just wrote, I realize that she is totally in control of our sex act. I'd just never thought of it that way. With the way we have sex, I feel like I could be anyone!

The impersonal, no-nonsense sex men described with their primary part-ners failed to provoke feelings of satiety. They also triggered men's fears about themselves as masculine enough, good enough. That's the crux of these narratives: Men worked very hard to ensure pleasure for their partners; tamped down their own preferences and desires so as to not make her uncomfortable; and took on their partner's failure to experience orgasm as their own failure. What they desired in return was a partner who expressed genuine interest, craving for, and delight in them. Yet that proved to be the very thing every man in this study reported that their primary partners withheld.

Their failure to evoke sexual desire and sexual pleasure within their primary partnership stood as an experience of failure and shame. Holden (41, married) said:

> [My wife] has never been able to orgasm by intercourse—and while I understand completely that this is a normal, and very common occurrence, there is a part of me (a small part) that wonders if I might not be able to bring her there if I could last long enough, or if she would consent to let me try this or that technique. I know that it's the societal pressure talking, but there is a small part of me that is disappointed and has to wonder if it might not be possible if only I were better, or if she was.

Thus, despite the knowledge that many women simply do not orgasm via intercourse, men still battled with the notion that this stood as their failure. Men spoke of researching sexual topics, especially women's orgasm (more on this in Chapter 6). Yet even knowing that inability to orgasm from penetrative intercourse alone exists as a typical experience failed to assuage concerns about what that lack said about them, as a man and a lover. Everett (42, married) added:

> My sex life at home is broken/failed. The majority of the problem is with me/my head. I'm bummed that my wife cannot have an orgasm by me, either orally or through intercourse. Though I've been reassured that this is not an uncommon problem, it is for me. And an orgasm happens so easily for me [that her lack of orgasm] bums me out.

When their efforts failed to induce their wife's orgasm, many men wrestled with guilt that their lack of prowess was at fault. This pressure to be "good at sex" and to evoke orgasms ran through the narratives. Within their marriages, this script proved damaging.

On one hand, we can commend these men on their concern for their partner's pleasure. They clearly showed concern for their partner's sexual experience, rather than feeling as though their orgasm eclipses all else. On the other, the focus on their partner's orgasm as a marker of their worth proves detrimental to their own sense of self-esteem. Current mainstream discourse proves replete with discussions of avoiding goal-oriented sex. At the same time, bookstores brim with self-help books focused on teaching men to generate a woman's orgasm (e.g., Kerner's *She Comes First*, Karp's *The Guide to Great Sex*). We cannot know their primary partners' feelings on this topic (i.e., whether they experienced their inorgasmic encounters as bothersome). However, for the men in this study, these experiences provoked shame and upset.

Men struggled with the rejection from their spouse. They assigned motives and intent to their primary partners' behaviors. For these men, all imagined roads led to the conclusion that they were simply not good enough. Sloan (36, married) explained:

> I know all relationships change with time, but I think making sure that your significant other knows you are still attracted to them, desire them, and appreciate them [should be standard]. I don't get that feeling in my marriage very often.

While media and commonsense narratives of men position them as purely interested in their own orgasms, these interviews challenged those assumptions. Men spoke of a desire to feel *wanted*, *desired*, and *valued* sexually. When they didn't feel that from their wives, they suffered. This echoes previous research which showed that while the majority of men in the sample espoused the traditional gendered ideas around sexuality (e.g., that men are the desirers rather than the ones being desired), nearly 40% of those men reported wanting to be desired by their partner (Masters, Casey, Wells, & Morrison, 2012). Another study found that men preferred a more egalitarian pattern of initiation of sexual activity because they wanted to be seen as an object of their partner's sexual desire (Dworkin & O'Sullivan, 2005). The men in this study valued their partners demonstrating desire and recognized initiating sexual activity as a means to accomplish this. Sloan (36, married) added:

> The first few years of our relationship I didn't mind always pursuing and initiating, but eventually it started taking its toll on me. I started feeling unattractive and undesirable. I resented my wife for making me feel so rejected. I felt selfish for letting the unhappiness of our sex life make me feel so crappy about myself and my marriage in general.

Men internalized the experience of always being the initiator of sex as an indicator that their spouse lacked genuine sexual interest in them. Men have reported similar sentiments in other studies (Elliott & Umberson, 2008; Montemurro & Riehman-Murphy, 2018). Interestingly, in my interviews with women in *The Secret Life of the Cheating Wife*, they reported this same reaction (Walker, 2018). In fact, research from 2019 found that participants reported that the sting of being rejected after an attempt to initiate sex lasted longer than the satisfaction of having a sexual advance accepted (Dobson, Zhu, Balzarini, & Campbell, 2019).

These narratives suggest that, at least for some of us, when relationship dynamics involve one partner constantly playing the initiator while the other simply waits to be approached, rejects the advances, or gives in as though sex is a "chore," the initiator grows resentful, and ultimately feels rejected. And yet most couples aren't having conversations about sexual preferences and expectations or negotiating initiation (Montemurro & Riehman-Murphy, 2018). It's common for couples to enter into marriage without explicitly discussing sexual preferences with regard to frequency, style, acts, etc. The assumption stands that "love" will work out sexual issues. Yet that's often not the case. Often these patterns exist prior to marriage and couples forge ahead with marriage only to see these conflicts grow rather than abate. For these men, the obvious dissatisfaction of their wives hindered their own satisfaction. This echoes a 2014 study which found that for husbands, high levels of relationship satisfaction correlates with their wives' reports of greater sexual satisfaction (Yoo, Bartle-Haring, Day, & Gangamma, 2014). Conversely, for wives, their husbands' sexual satisfaction fails to correlate with their relationship satisfaction. This could be tied to the demands of masculinity, which require men to demonstrate prowess as evidenced through his partner's orgasm.

Outside Partners Make Me "Feel Less Sexually Defective"

For many men, finding an outside partner helped alleviate some of the hurt of their wives' rejection. Patrick (33, married) said:

> My wife has never enjoyed intercourse personally and would rather the event be over as soon as possible. I use[d] to think this was some fault of mine: [that] I was just a horrible lover or something, but my [outside partner] has put those thoughts to rest.

Notice Patrick's initial assumption is that his wife's failure to enjoy sex must be due to his lack of skill. Having another partner who enjoyed sex meant the fault lay not with him. There's no consideration of the possibility that one person may be a great sexual fit with one partner and not with another. In these men's minds, this is all very black and white, and blame for sex that fails to be mutually enjoyed must be assessed to someone. They tended to blame themselves until an outside partner enjoyed sex with them. Then they shifted blame to their primary partner. Since under their framework sex between two people that fails to satisfy both parties must be blamed on someone, better the blame lay with their primary partners than with themselves.

For these men, having a partner who enjoyed sex and with whom they could demonstrate their sexual prowess—and by extension their masculinity—proved healing. Matteo (44, married) explained the vast impact of his outside partner in flowery language:

> I did not know what [a woman's orgasm] even looked like until I'd been splashed in the face, or felt the quiver of a Kegel muscles strangle my masculinity, or the amazing feeling of warm rivers of my partner's nectar flow from her flower as we undulate in an entangled hot mess of intertwined arms and legs. From full body contact spooning to nonstop exploration through the gliding of my hands and gentle yet powerful control of my [outside partner's] body through a firm grip by the roots of her hair... These are the things that do not happen at home because they are not received well.

Matteo waxed poetically about sexual encounters with his outside partner, but notice his positioning of himself in that description. He is "powerful" and in "control" of his partner's body. The men of this study absolutely defined themselves by their sexual performance.

Their primary partners' rejection of sensuality and protracted sexual encounters hurt the men in this study deeply. They experienced this as a rejection of their sexual skills and acumen. Nowhere in the narratives do men consider some other explanation for their primary partners' (perceived) disinterest *except* faulting themselves. If it's their fault, then their masculinity isn't intact. The sexual dynamics of their primary partnerships threatened their sense of themselves as manly, which gravely hurt their self-esteem. This proved problematic and detrimental to their primary partnerships and their relationships with others.

Thus, the positive response of their outside partner soothed fears that the fault for the lack of sexual response from their wives rested with them. Having a woman who enjoyed sex with them, who actively participated, and anticipated seeing them for the sex served as an antidote to the years of shame regarding their marital sex lives. Sloan (36, married) explained, "The biggest thing I get from my outside relationship is feeling desired and attractive. And that I don't get resentful in my marriage." The sexual dynamics in their primary partnerships led to men resenting their primary partners. Resentment came up in *The Secret Life of the Cheating Wife* as well. Women reported resentment because of unfair divisions of labor and having to go without orgasms (Walker, 2018), but they also grew resentful of the lack of satisfying sex within their primary partnerships. Likewise, these men grew resentful because of what they believed their primary partner's lack of interest in sex said about them. However, their resentment rested in their belief that their primary partner's lack of interest meant they weren't manly enough.

An outside partner stood as a symbol of men's ability to be "great in bed," something they valued and served as evidence of their manliness. This provided much-needed validation of their masculinity, which helped them feel better about themselves. Barry (37, married) explained:

Sometimes I feel like [my penis is] short, but [outside partner] claims different. She always tells me I am great and she has orgasms, and I know she does. Since I let go of my anxiety, I feel less frustrated with pleasing her. I know she gets pleasure, so each sexual encounter with her is exciting.

Notice that for Barry, what makes the encounters exciting is his ability to provoke orgasm in his partner. Absent is discussion of his own pleasure. His concerns center upon his own fitness as a sexual partner, his prowess, his penis size, his masculinity. His outside partner allays his fears that he is not enough (e.g., not big enough, not skilled enough, not desirable enough) both through her words (e.g., she tells him that his penis is adequate in length) and her actions, specifically her orgasm and his confidence that she isn't faking. For the men in this study, the value of sex with their outside partners lies in its ability to substantiate their masculinity. The legitimation of their status as manly provides their enjoyment and pleasure. These relationships served as outlets to redeem their sense of competence. Day-to-day life with a partner whom they perceived as caring so little about sex with them or about them as people took a toll on the men's sense of themselves as masculine. Outside partnerships existed as spaces where a sexual partner showed interest and desire, and provided praise for men's sexual efforts and accomplishments. Both served as confirmation of their masculinity, something they greatly needed for their self-esteem. For these men, their sense of their own masculinity remained bound up in their sexual performance and desirability.

Men's participation in outside partnerships improved their sense of confidence. Given the mandate of hegemonic masculinity in the United States includes sexual prowess, this is perhaps not surprising. Riley (39, married) also points out the importance of an emotional connection with a partner as the key to his top sexual performance. As mentioned in the previous chapter, many men in this inquiry believed an emotional connection was necessary for their best performance. He explained:

Knowing that I am not sexually defective—that everything actually still works the way it should (when the emotional context is there)—it makes me believe in myself a lot more. The more I believe, the more I care about myself. I have embraced other changes in my life as a result. Making a needed vehicle change, wardrobe upgrade, allowing myself rewards for things well done. These are all big steps towards the person I want to be.

For these men, knowing they were capable of quality sexual performance that provoked orgasm in their partner improved their sense of self. Ultimately, having a woman in their lives who consistently communicated (in a way these men could recognize) interest in them as both a lover and a person helped them feel better about themselves. Sloan (36, married) said:

I didn't realize how much my sex life was tied into my sense of self until I started an affair and realized how unhappy I had been in that regard. Naturally that puts me in a better mood and makes all my interactions more positive. I smile more, laugh more, and help put other people in better moods as well. When I felt more down about myself and how undesirable I felt to my wife, it just seemed to drain the energy from me.

Sloan realized the deep impact of his confidence in his sexual prowess. The feeling of being sexually desired by a woman proved impactful.

Ultimately, outside partnerships helped bolster fragile egos, which suffered for years under the weight of perceived constant rejection and failure as a lover. Having a partner who provided praise, compliments, and reassurance of their sexual prowess served as a much-needed boost. Rudy (42, married) explained:

I also discovered a side benefit in the way of ego boosts. This mainly consisted of compliments from the outside partner relating to either my skill, assets, or both. How much of that was true and how much was simple flattery/being nice, I have no way to know or evaluate, except in the cases of a partner where we had more than one meeting, so between the two of us we were both doing things that the other liked and wanted more of. I do think that the fact that I liked to make sure my partner was satisfied played a part in those compliments.

Notice Rudy questions the veracity of the flattery. For him, an outside partner's willingness to meet again and again held more weight than the compliments alone, although he certainly treasured the compliments. Despite the substantial pressure to perform sexually with outside partners or risk never getting another chance (discussed in Chapter 7), the payoff proved enormous.

Outside Partners Take the Pressure Off Primary Partners

With their sense of themselves as masculine and desired intact, men could better perform at home. Riley (39, married) remarked:

> If anything, it allows me to treat my spouse kinder, more patiently, understandingly, because I am feeling much better about my life and myself, and there is nothing for me to hold against my wife. It's not [my wife's] responsibility anymore, that section of her role has simply been outsourced. It removes a lot of friction and emotional baggage and makes everyday life much easier.

Men spoke of feeling more capable of exercising tolerance at home with their primary partners as a result of their outside partnerships. They described themselves as more able to let small things go and more likely to use healthy conflict resolution techniques. Greg (53, married) said, "I think I am more accepting of the marriage when I am in a relationship. There is some source of affection and intimacy, so I am not as resentful." Resentment came up again and again in these narratives. When men felt they went without intimacy, they felt anger toward their primary partner. Patrick (33, married) added, "Well, of course at some point it might be the undoing of the marriage, but on a day-to-day basis it allows me to not get frustrated about things that are lacking in the relationship at home." This sense of outside partnerships as a stopgap came up again and again. Greg (53, married) said, "There is an ego boost/confidence boost that comes with knowing you are still attractive to the opposite sex that extends to other parts of my life." Men spoke of the ways outside partnerships helped in tamping down frustration at home. Sloan (36, married) described the impact of his outside partnership:

> I used to try a lot of romantic gestures aimed at making my wife happy, and with the hope of it leading to sex. I used to get so frustrated and feel so rejected when my attempts didn't lead anywhere. I now have an outside relationship that satisfies that need and therefore takes the friction out of that aspect of my marital relationship. I feel happier and more…whole. I'm not as easily frustrated by little things. Having that outside partner is a stress relief in a lot of ways. It makes the little stresses in my marriage easier to let go of, which probably makes me more fun to be around!

Again here, we see men applying existing social scripts in the hopes that they will work (i.e., result in an interest in sex with them on the part of their primary partner). Again, we see the script failing. Outside partners helped mitigate the hurt and frustration of failing scripts.

The ability to let go of resentment and frustration due to outside partners came up repeatedly. Men spoke of displaying more kindness and patience at home. Riley (39, married) added:

> In some ways it makes it easier for me to enjoy my wife as a friend and partner, since I am being fulfilled emotionally and sexually elsewhere. It allows me to be patient and kind and caring without having to get past those feelings of rejection and assorted emotional baggage first.

When men's fears about their masculinity quieted, they believed themselves better partners at home. The increased capacity to manage frustration gained from outside partnerships came up repeatedly in these narratives. Men believed life before outside partners to be intolerable. For many men, outside partnerships and primary partnerships combined to meet all of their needs. Gus (62, married) described his life:

> My outside partner provides the intimacy, excitement, and friendship, while my wife provides stability, family ties, and companionship. When I have an OP, I find my relationship with my spouse to be much more easygoing because the desire for sex is satisfied for me. I can focus on

being a friend and good partner to my spouse without the frustration of insufficient intimacy.

Gus describes the need to have multiple women in his life to fulfill all of his needs. This sentiment echoed the findings of my previous study of women participating in outside partnerships. Again, we see the Infidelity Workaround at play: folks outsourcing unmet needs to an interested third party. With both groups (the women from the previous book and the men in this inquiry), successful outsourcing led to a shift in perspectives regarding relationships. Specifically, many espoused the belief that perhaps having multiple people in your life to address different sets of needs existed as necessary.

A couple of the narratives read much darker. Two men in the study spoke of deep-seated anger, frustration, and resentment. Donald (61, married) said:

> These feelings of hatred for myself and [my wife] would surface time and time again because I felt that once again she was denying me pleasure or the opportunity to seek pleasure elsewhere; but felt upset [that I had to] leav[e] my home to seek that pleasure. This created an uncomfortable and unwieldy dichotomy.

Another man intimated domestic violence, or the possibility that it might occur. Clay (46, married) explained, "[When not in an outside partnership] my temper is quicker and I'm more likely to be violent when pushed." When asked directly about incidents of domestic violence in his current primary partnership, Clay denied any such events. He clarified that he believed himself capable of violence when pushed, which is part of what motivated him to seek outside partnerships to bridge the gaps in his marriage to avoid incidents of violence. In his mind, his participation in outside partnerships prevented his perpetration of domestic violence.

Outside Partners Reduces Burden on Spouses

Men reported a reduced burden on their spouse as another benefit enjoyed as a result of outside partnerships. Specifically, they claimed they stopped "bothering" their wives for sexual interaction, which they believed she had no interest in. Again, we cannot know how their wives feel about this, nor can we know if the men's perceptions of their situations accurately reflect the circumstances. The narratives reflect the men's perceptions of their primary partnerships, which function to them as fact and reality. Tucker (60, married) added, "It has relieved the pressure that I used to put on my wife to be more sexually active." Ultimately, men believed their primary partners benefitted from the arrangement. Sloan (36, married) added:

> Before I decided to have an affair, I was literally having conversations with myself about whether not being happy was a legitimate reason to get a divorce. It was agonizing in many ways. When I finally gave myself permission to have an affair it took all the pressure off my marriage to satisfy my sexual desires.

The men believed their outside partnerships essentially served as a way to outsource certain aspects of their marriages. This echoed the findings in my study with women who participated in outside partnerships, who openly spoke of outsourcing the sex in their marriages (Walker, 2018). However, most of those women participated in highly bounded relationships where the sole purpose was sexual pleasure. Like the seven women in that study who outsourced the emotional aspect of their primary partnerships, these men described outside relationships with what they believed to be an "emotional intimacy" component. Additionally, these men benefitted most from the validation of their masculinity provided by their outside partnerships.

These men believed that their primary partners also gained much from the men's participation in outside partnerships. Byron (57, married) said:

So, by me finding some other partners to fulfill my desires, I don't need to bother her with frequent requests. She doesn't feel the pressure to have sex just to satisfy me and I don't feel like I need to bother her for it as often. So, it's kind of a win-win situation.

With the pressure off, men could shift their focus. Patrick (33, married) added:

I use to study and think about how to "win my wife back," but now I just go about life with a little less worry. When I'm in an OP [outside partnership], I'm not at all interested [in] attempting to repair my relationship with my wife. Which probably isn't good for the marriage, but at least I'm more satisfied. And in that place of satisfaction I think I'm easier going on my spouse. I don't ask her for things now that I know she doesn't want to give, and she is happier for it.

Patrick believed his wife happier with the new circumstances, but he had not asked her. Like most of the men in this inquiry, husbands assumed their wives' feelings and thoughts without confirming them through conversation and inquiry. Patrick provided an example of how things once worked in his marriage.

For example, when we were younger, she dressed a tad attractive. Now she doesn't work and mainly wears men's gym shorts and shirts. It used to bother me and I use to nag her about it, asking her to kinda try a bit. It doesn't bother me as much now, and I've stopped the bad habit of mentioning that she dresses very unattractively. For now, [my] need for an attractive companion is satisfied elsewhere and my wife is happy to be free of my nagging too.

Due to Patrick's participation in outside partnerships, he stopped disparaging his wife's wardrobe choices. Let's unpack this a bit. Men spoke of frustration with their wives, who they believed lost interest in passion, sex, provision of relational management, and the men as individuals with needs. Patrick's approach to this dilemma included insulting his wife's appearance and telling her that her clothes were unattractive. As a result of Patrick's time spent with an outside partner, he altered his approach.

> So, in short, while I've been in this outside relationship, I've been more able to bear the frustrations of a home life that is very unsatisfying and just focus on the things I need to do for the kids. She is ironically very much happier also in the marriage since I met my friend. She probably doesn't know why, but she's glad I don't care anymore.

For these men, outside partners demonstrated passion and sexual desire for them as lovers in part by dressing up for meetings. For many men in this study, women dressing in clothing traditionally regarded as feminine equated to sexual interest in them and desire for them. They expressed upset with primary partners who failed to present themselves as aesthetically pleasing (e.g., hair removal and feminine clothing) and ready for sex. The men internalized their failure to do so as a rejection of them as sexual partners, and a rejection of them as masculine. Only a few men admitted to nagging and insulting their wife's appearance. These descriptions illustrate how tethered these men were to gender norms, expectations, and scripts.

Given that men relied upon their wives to manage their emotional lives through relational management, dealing with chronic feelings of frustration and upset at the perceived loss of sexual interest on their wives' part and the accompanying feelings of emasculation proved extremely difficult. Given their socialization to wait for their wife to ask about their feelings only to have her never ask, the pain they perceived her to be inflicting proved too much. Outside partners helped because they soothed men's frustrations. Rudy (42, married) "Probably a 6-year period where having an OP [outside partner] kept life calm and not having one had me on edge." All of that translated to better behavior at home. Travis (43, married) added, "I no longer worry (care?) about some of the insignificant annoyances at home because I know in the overall picture they don't matter." The men in this study truly believed the validation gained from outside partnerships functioned as critical in their lives.

Men spoke about functioning as better fathers and better partners as a result of their outside partnerships. Marcello (44, married) explained:

My outside relationship has made me a better father and even more attentive husband because I can focus on her emotional needs and not expect repayment in the form of sex. My therapy goes well, my kids get played with, my wife has a husband who puts dishes away and takes out the garbage. In turn, she is happy because I am listening instead of being in sex fantasy land. The chores are done which makes her feel validated. It makes me a better partner. When those desires are not met, I spend a large portion of my mental time thinking and plotting on how to have sex. I can be with my kids, at the store or even watching tv with my family but inside I am spinning and plotting on how to one day have a sexual experience again. I get more stressed, less involved with the family. I pay attention less to their needs because [I] am not happy.

Men openly admitted that without this validation, they performed poorly as partners and parents. Notice Marcello admits that all he can think about is his unmet needs. He couches the need as sex, but as we've seen, sex isn't just sex for these men. Sex includes enthusiastic sensuality (discussed in Chapter 6) and caring.

These findings challenge the current understandings of men in intimate relationships, which posits that men's interest as purely sexual pleasure while women value emotional intimacy and validation (Hook, Gerstein, & Gridley, 2003; Vohs, Catanese, & Baumeister, 2004). In fact, Leticia Peplau found in 2001 that women expressed a greater desire for more emotional intimacy (Peplau, 2001). Women work harder to generate emotional intimacy through sharing and urging communication (Elliott & Umberson, 2008; Rubin, 1990). However, multiple studies examining men's perceptions and experiences with sex workers found that for regular customers, while the men still enjoy the sexual release, the objective of the association becomes what they perceive as emotional intimacy (Bernstein, 2007; Lever & Dolnick, 2000; Plumridge, Chetwynd, Reed, & Gifford, 1997; Sanders, 2008). Research shows that men highly value the emotional intimacy of intimate relationships, especially as they age (Sandberg, 2013; Seal & Ehrhardt, 2003). The findings of this study support that research.

Conclusion

The dynamics of their sexual relationships with their primary partners functioned as a source of self-doubt and frustration. Men complained of feelings of being undesirable and lacking adequate prowess. This combined with the lack of relational management provided by primary partners led men to outsource to a more interested third party as part of an Infidelity Workaround. The men in this study realized their sense of themselves as worthy hinged on how the women in their lives regarded them. Because of this, they regarded their primary partners' withholding of praise and sexual enthusiasm as particularly cruel. They believed that outside partnerships helped soothe the hurts of their primary partnerships by addressing their unmet needs for praise and validation. Other people in their lives noticed their heightened sense of self as a result. Men believed that outside partnerships helped alleviate burdens for their primary partners. Further, they perceived themselves as more capable primary partners due to the salve of outside partnerships.

References

Alksnis, C., Desmarais, S., & Woods, E. (1996). Gender differences in scripts for different kinds of dates. *Sex Roles, 34*(5/6), 331–336. https://doi.org/10.1007/bf01547805.

Bachen, C., & Illouz, E. (1995). Imagining romance: Young people's cultural models of romance and love. *Critical Studies in Media Communication, 13*(4), 279–308. https://doi.org/10.1080/15295039609366983.

Bachen, C. M., & Illouz, E. (1996). Imagining romance: Young people's cultural models of romance and love. *Critical Studies in Mass Communication, 13*(4), 279–308. https://doi.org/10.1080/15295039609366983.

Bernstein, E. (2007). *Temporarily yours: Intimacy, authenticity, and the commerce of sex*. Chicago, IL: University of Chicago Press.

Dobson, K., Zhu, J., Balzarini, R. N., & Campbell, L. (2019). *Responses to sexual advances and satisfaction in romantic relationships: Is yes good and no bad?* https://doi.org/10.31234/osf.io/p9nc8.

Duncombe, J., & Marsden, D. (1993). Love and intimacy: The gender division of emotion and 'emotion work': A neglected aspect of sociological discussion of heterosexual relationships. *Sociology, 27*(2), 221–241.

Dworkin, S. L., & O'Sullivan, L. (2005). Actual versus desired initiation patterns among a sample of college men: Tapping disjunctures within traditional male sexual scripts. *The Journal of Sex Research, 42*(2), 150–158. https://doi.org/10.1080/00224490509552268.

Elliott, S., & Umberson, D. (2008). The performance of desire: Gender and sexual negotiation in long-term marriages. *Journal of Marriage and Family, 70*(2), 391–406. https://doi.org/10.1111/j.1741-3737.2008.00489.x.

Gabb, J. (2019). The relationship work of sexual intimacy in long-term heterosexual and LGBTQ partnerships. *Current Sociology.* https://doi.org/10.1177/0011392119826619.

Hockey, J., Meah, A., & Robinson, V. (2012). *Mundane heterosexualities: From theory to practices.* Basingstoke: Palgrave Macmillan.

Hook, M. K., Gerstein, L. H., & Gridley, L. D. B. (2003). How close are we? Measuring intimacy and examining gender differences. *Journal of Counseling and Development, 81*(4), 462–472. https://doi.org/10.1002/j.1556-6678.2003.tb00273.x.

Kim, J. L., Sorsoli, C. L., Collins, K., Zylbergold, B. A., Schooler, D., & Tolman, D. L. (2007). From sex to sexuality: Exposing the heterosexual script on primetime network television. *The Journal of Sex Research, 44*(2), 145–157.

Lever, J., & Dolnick, D. (2000). Clients and call girls: Seeking sex and intimacy. In R. Weitzer (Ed.), *Sex for sale: Prostitution, pornography, and the sex industry* (pp. 85–100). London: Routledge.

Lodge, A., & Umberson, D. (2012). All shook up: Sexuality of mid- to later life married couples. *Journal of Marriage and Family, 74*(3), 428–443. https://doi.org/10.1111/j.1741-3737.2012.00969.x.

Lorber, J. (2005). *Breaking the bowls: Degendering and feminist change.* New York: W. W. Norton.

Masters, T., Casey, E. A., Wells, E. A., & Morrison, D. M. (2012). Sexual scripts among young heterosexually active men and women: Continuity and change. *The Journal of Sex Research, 50*(5), 409–420. https://doi.org/10.1080/00224499.2012.661102.

Montemurro, B., & Riehman-Murphy, C. (2018). Ready and waiting: Heterosexual men's decision-making narratives in initiation of sexual intimacy. *Men & Masculinities.* https://doi.org/10.1177/1097184X17753040.

Paik, A., & Woodley, V. (2005). *Scripting romance in adolescence: Preferences and predictors in the sequencing of ideal dating relationships.* Paper presented at the American Sociological Association, Philadelphia, PA.

Peplau, L. A. (2001). Rethinking women's sexual orientation: An interdisciplinary, relationship-focused approach. *Personal Relationships, 8*(1), 1–19. https://doi.org/10.1111/j.1475-6811.2001.tb00025.x.

Plumridge, E., Chetwynd, J., Reed, A., & Gifford, S. (1997). Discourses of emotionality in commercial sex: The missing client voice. *Feminism and Psychology, 7*(2), 165–181.

Rose, S., & Frieze, I. H. (1993). Young singles' contemporary dating scripts. *Sex Roles, 28*(9/10), 499–509. https://doi.org/10.1007/bf00289677.

Rubin, L. B. (1990). *Men and women together.* New York: Harper Perennial.

Sandberg, L. J. (2013). Just feeling a naked body close to you: Men, sexuality and intimacy in later life. *Sexualities, 16*(3–4), 261–282. https://doi.org/10.1177/1363460713481726.

Sanders, T. (2008). Male sexual scripts: Intimacy, sexuality and pleasure in the purchase of commercial sex. *Sociology, 42*(3), 400–417. https://doi.org/10.1177/0038038508088833.

Seal, D. W., & Ehrhardt, A. A. (2003). Masculinity and urban men: Perceived scripts for courtship, romantic, and sexual interactions with women. *Culture Health & Sexuality Health & Sexuality, 4,* 295–319. https://doi.org/10.1080/136910501171698.

Simon, W., & Gagnon, J. H. (1984). Sexual scripts. *Society, 22*(1), 53–60.

Simon, W., & Gagnon, J. H. (2003). Sexual scripts: Origins, influences and changes. *Qualitative Sociology, 26*(4), 491–497. https://doi.org/10.1023/b:quas.0000005053.99846.e5.

Vohs, K. D., Catanese, K. R., & Baumeister, R. F. (2004). Sex in "his" versus "her" relationships. In J. H. Harvey, A. Wenzel, & S. Sprecher (Eds.), *The handbook of sexuality in close relationships* (pp. 455–474). Mahwah, NJ: Lawrence Erlbaum Associates Publishers.

Walker, A. M. (2018). *The secret life of the cheating wife: Power, pragmatism, and pleasure in women's infidelity.* Lanham, MD: Lexington Books.

Yoo, H., Bartle-Haring, S., Day, R. D., & Gangamma, R. (2014). Couple communication, emotional and sexual intimacy, and relationship satisfaction. *Journal of Sex and Marital Therapy, 40*(4), 275–293. https://doi.org/10.1080/0092623X.2012.751072.

6

"I Seek a Partner Who Actually Wants Me to Make Up for Lost Time": The Girlfriend Experience in Outside Partnerships Helps Reduce FOMO

Introduction

Men spoke about the contrast between the encounters in their outside partnerships and the experiences within their primary partnerships. Specifically, men reported rushed sexual encounters within their primary partnerships. Their perception of a lack of interest from their primary partners in leisurely, sensual encounters proved hurtful to these men. Thus, within their outside partnerships, they sought experiences more like what popular culture refers to as "The Girlfriend Experience" (Sanders, 2008). Deep kissing, lingering touch, and "taking your time" delineate the Girlfriend Experience from a more rushed encounter. These men often interpreted their partner's preference for a rushed encounter as disinterest in them as a sexual partner. Their outside partnerships offered leisurely, sensual encounters, which the men internalized as validation of them as a sexual partner, and sexual desire for them specifically. The men held the experience of feeling desired in high regard and importance. The men in this study framed the importance regarding the loss of satisfying sex not through the lens of the loss of pleasure, but the loss of their sense of themselves as masculine. The narratives revolved

© The Author(s) 2020
A. M. Walker, *Chasing Masculinity*,
https://doi.org/10.1007/978-3-030-49818-4_6

upon the ways that their primary partners' disinterest in sensual encounters with them made them feel less than manly. Interestingly, this finding stands in contrast to most of the interviews with women, which focused on loss of sexual pleasure in their marriages. Most of the women I spoke with pursued affairs solely for sexual pleasure. The men in this inquiry talked more at length about the loss of their sense of themselves as a manly individual.

Men in this study reported deep-seated insecurities about their own worth and their manliness. This functions as a result of the inherent instability of masculinity, a status that can never be awarded permanently, but must be reified routinely. Some of the men's backgrounds worked to feed those insecurities. Roughly a third (15) of the men in this study described themselves as sexually inexperienced before marriage. Given masculinity's requirement that men rack up high partner counts, this inexperience worked to feed doubt. Add that lack of experience to the marital sexual dynamics nearly every man I spoke with detailed, and men's self-doubt regarding their sexual prowess stands illuminated. Given the average age of the men in this study was nearly 46, it's perhaps unsurprising that the men expressed a sense of FOMO (fear of missing out). They talked about concerns that life was "passing them by" and worries that they had not exercised enough of the sexual and romantic opportunities presented to them. Outside partnerships existed as a way to mitigate those feelings.

The Girlfriend Experience

Experiences with outside partners stood in sharp contrast to their marriages. Many men in this study mentioned that the chief difference between their outside partnerships and their primary partnerships was sensual, extended encounters. This echoes the literature looking at the "Girlfriend Experience," which refers to a kind of unhurried, sensual sexual experience men purchase from sex workers. Much like the men in Teela Sanders' (2008) study, the sexual facet of the outside partnership functioned as an extra benefit. Regarding the sexual activity within their outside partnerships, the men appreciated the "Girlfriend Experience," a popular culture term meaning sexual encounters including "kissing, caressing, and other sensual acts (rather than brief sex acts)" (Sanders, 2008, p. 407).

Outside Partners Provide "The Girlfriend Experience"

Men spoke at length about their frustration with their primary partner's disinterest in prolonged, unrushed, sensual sexual encounters (discussed in previous chapters). Men highly valued the emotional connection, emotional intimacy, and relational support outside partners provided. While certainly sexual, the Girlfriend Experience also provided validation and a boost to their perceived self-esteem. Patrick (33, married) explained, "Selfishly an outside partnership helps quiet those dumb little teenage voices in all our heads that tell us we are dumb, ugly, and unlikable. If left up to only how my wife makes me feel…" The Girlfriend Experience provided by outside partners helped mitigate the way their "failures" at home wore on them. Rudy (42, married) echoed this sentiment:

> My wife was pregnant with our second child and was not interested in sex. She would make herself available for sex if I asked, but it always seemed like a chore for her. Basically, she wanted me in and done.

For men who wanted more than anything to be desired by their partner, a spouse who approached sex as just another household chore proved hurtful and damaging. This challenged the relationship dynamics as well as the men's sense of self-esteem. The loss of sexual pleasure proved taxing, but the lack of feeling desired was much more salient, especially given the men's internalization of this as a statement about their masculinity.

After enduring years of sexless marriages, or marriages where their wives viewed sex as a chore, these men reveled in their outside partnerships. Simon (39, married) described this sensation:

> I was lying awake in bed the other night thinking about this. In my primary relationship right now, I get a daily kiss on the cheek. I try to cuddle in bed. I give backrubs. I give hugs, but I don't get anything in return. I like the passion and foreplay of my outside partnership and the sense of desire it gives me. I think primarily I get passion. Passion and kissing. I like to kiss, cuddle, just show affection in a physical way.

Men admitted that the perception of a lack of desire on the part of their primary partner decreased their sense of their self-esteem. An outside partnership worked as a balm against the hurts inflicted within their marriages. The way their outside partners made them feel about themselves served as the primary trait sought. Patrick explained:

> My OP is no track star, flat-bellied model. I just wanted a partner who just liked me physically... even a little. Interestingly, my [outside partner] takes a lot of responsibility [for] the quality of [our] sexual encounters, not out of obligation, but out of selfish enjoyment. She works hard at making it fun for HERself, which is what I've always wanted.

Patrick appreciates that his partner actively constructs her own orgasm out of "selfish enjoyment." Notice that contrary to popular conceptions of affairs in the United States, the men admitted that physicality wasn't the primary trait they sought in an outside partner. Rather, enthusiasm and desire proved more important. The men internalized their outside partner's enjoyment of sex as proof of their own sexual desirability, which bolstered their sense of themselves as masculine.

Unpacking Patrick's statement further, his sentiment that he sought someone who "liked" him "even a little" proves heartbreaking. The men in this study expressed a belief that their primary partners stopped "liking" them. In my previous book, women reported an initial phase of questioning their own desirability in response to their primary partners withholding sex. But few spoke of concerns about their primary partners "liking" them. (Those that did described extremely unhealthy, toxic, and abusive relationships.) Men's concerns about their primary partners "liking" them calls to mind a statement made by Jon Cryer's character, Alan, on *Two and Half Men* (a show no longer broadcasting new episodes, but still playing in syndication nearly daily). Alan explains to his brother in

Season 3, Episode 10, "With every woman I've ever met, I have twisted myself into knots just trying to get them to like me." While it is easy to wave our hands and say, "it's just television," we have to remember that "television both shapes and reflects American culture" (Foss, 2008, p. 43) and can reveal the cultural context of the times. Further, television portrayals serve us an "array of masculinities" (Feasey, 2008, p. 3). Television shows serve as scripts and models for us to draw upon within our relationships (Bachen & Illouz, 1995; Gerbner, Gross, Morgan, Signorielli, & Shanahan, 2002). Alan's character stands in juxtaposition to his brother, Charlie's, more hegemonic presentations of masculinity (e.g., womanizing, resisting both emotional attachments and discussions of feelings). He enacts a more beta masculinity, in part because of his inability to enact a hegemonic one (Walker, 2014). Alan's concerns that he does everything he can to get the women in his life to "like" him may ring true for many viewers. The show ran twelve seasons and earned millions per episode. It's fair to say it was "popular." Alan goes on to explain: "My education, my job, my clothes, my car, my very behavior, all chosen simply to get women to approve of me." Charlie asks: "And how's that worked out for you?" Alan responds: "They don't approve of me." While watching the episode and accompanying laugh track, the viewer is supposed to chuckle at Alan's disclosure and his attitude. However, one cannot help but feel sympathetic toward someone who admits that everything in their life is bent on getting women to "like" them, and yet all their efforts failed. And so it is with these narratives. It would be easy to wave these men's accounts away, but they reveal a deep and abiding pain, hurt, and frustration that nothing they've done has produced the desired effort. And at the end of the day, all they want is to be "liked" by their romantic partner. Under that lens, we understand that these outside partnerships existed as spaces of healing.

Outside partnerships provided the Girlfriend Experience, making true men's fantasies of having a willing and interested sexual partner, a condition that not only validates their masculinity, but improves their sense of self-esteem. The appeal of their affairs rested not in variety or alleviating boredom, but in meeting their need to be desired. Additionally, their outside partners tended to view sex quite differently than their wives. This created the circumstances for the kind of sex men desired and which helped soothe their hurt feelings from their perception of their primary partner's disinterest. Sloan (36, married) added,

> Most women I've talked to when looking for an outside partner are much more sexually aware than my wife. It makes it easier to relax and have fun. And sex should be fun, right? I'm very focused on making my outside partner happy when we're together. Whether that means physically through massage, foreplay, sex, etc., or making her laugh, enjoying our conversation, etc. Since time is always limited, I really want to make sure she enjoys herself and her time with me.

Men framed an outside partner's sexual self-awareness as desire for them and validation of them as a sexual partner. The more their partners enjoyed sex with them, the more the men in this study reported feeling desired. They worked very hard to ensure their partners enjoyed themselves in hopes of having more opportunities to continue the relationship with their outside partner (More on this in Chapter 7). Further, their outside partner's willingness to engage in prolonged, sensual activities (e.g., massage, foreplay, extended time lying in bed together) helped boost men's sense of their self-esteem, but also provided emotional healing. These men highly valued their outside partner's performance of desire for them.

"Prioritize Sex with Me"

In outside partnerships, their partners showed genuine interest, which paved the way to share sexual preferences. The men in this study admit that attention from their female partners is crucial to their sense of themselves as men, as masculine beings. Within outside partnerships, men felt wanted, desired, and accepted. These relationships served their need for validation, attention, and praise. More importantly, their behaviors indicated they prioritized the men as sexual partners, which the men highly valued. Marcello (44, married) said:

With kids pulling on my wife's legs, even if I do look at her with a cfm [come fuck me] look, there is no action. On the contrary, my lover called the sitter, waxed her pussy and made a point to be ready. Even if I say to my wife, "Hey, Wednesday night let's do popcorn, movie, and a vibrator," there will be a catch or a reason why not to do so. For my wife, the mother role takes precedence over the lover and wife role.

Notice Marcello equates his outside partner's preparation for sexual activity with being prioritized. In reality, his outside partner may not think much about him or prioritize him at all. Her extent of thought about him may actually be limited to the time needed to prep for sexual activity. For her, he may function as a small concern in the grand scheme of things. However, because she cleared her schedule to meet for sex and prepared her body to be aesthetically pleasing to him, in his mind, he's a priority for her.

Many men in this inquiry reported this sentiment. Thus, it's entirely possible that their primary partners routinely do things to prioritize these men, but the men fail to experience those acts as such. Regardless of what their primary partners did, felt, or intended, these men only recognized enthusiasm and interest in them as a sexual partner as an act of making them a priority. For these men, the social mandate of sexual prowess as a marker of masculinity impacted their experiences of intimate relationships. Given their narrow view of what constitutes "prioritizing" your partner, their primary partners may engage in a host of caring actions to communicate the men's importance and priority in their lives. However, the men can't experience those activities as such. Marcello fails to look at his wife's parenting responsibilities and consider that perhaps she both prioritizes and desires him, yet also lacks the energy to act on that. Instead, he problematizes her feelings about him, and assumes she simply lacks interest in him and that he isn't a priority for her. Not feeling prioritized cut the men deeply. They spoke with animosity and cynicism about where they ranked on their wives' list of priorities—where they perceived themselves to rank. Like the minority of women in *The Secret Life of the Cheating Wife* also outsourcing the emotional aspect of their primary

partnerships to an interested third party, affairs functioned for validation, attention, and being cared for rather than being about orgasms and
sexual pleasure (Walker, 2018).

Interestingly, Patrick (33, married) expressed the belief that men's
bodies simply lack appeal in our culture. He relayed a recent conversation
at a race with fellow runners.

> People like to see women in tight clothes. Then why don't men wear tight
> running clothes? The moment I asked this aloud the women in the group
> nearly barfed. The male body is oddly one of the most disgusting things
> to a woman, and that has always been odd to me. Is the pressure on
> women to perform sexually causing women to dislike men sexually? Or
> is it the other way around? Is pressure being placed on women because
> they tend to not enjoy a man's body at all, and men are trying to pressure
> them into "better" sex through other influences of society? Why don't
> women like men's bodies?

The experience of having the person who promised to cherish them
above all reject them repeatedly, and consistently lack any interest in
them as a sexual being struck at the core of their confidence and self-
esteem. For Patrick, the entire culture seems to be communicating a
rejection of men as sexually desirable, attractive, or pleasing to behold.
He hears that message more saliently due to being in a primary partnership where that sentiment is regularly communicated. Thus, his
perception that his primary partner fails to prioritize sexual activity with
him carries more weight and hurt. Correspondingly, an outside partner
who shows interest and desire for him helps quiet his concerns.

Feel Desired

Sexual scripts for men position them as the desire*r* rather than the desire*d*
(Wiederman, 2005). In our society, men play the role of pursuer, the
party expressing desire for their partner. Rarely do we present men as
desirable. For the men in this study, feeling that their partner had no
real interest in them hurt. Mitch (59, married) said, "All I want is what I

consider to be a 'normal' sex life. I guess I just want to feel wanted, to boil it down to its essence." This sentiment proved common. The idea that the kind of sex they desired was "normal" and that their primary partnerships lacked "normal" sex fueled the idea of missing out. Outside partners who express their desire for them boost men's self-perception. Aiden (31, married) explained, "I work hard to stay in shape. And to hear a beautiful woman say, 'damn how does your wife not rip your clothes off?' is a good feeling." Outside partners' vocalization that their primary partners' disinterest in them stood as "their loss" proved important. Men interpreted their perception of their primary partners' disinterest in them—as evidenced by a failure to engage in extended sessions—as a statement regarding their own lack of worth. Thus, having an outside partner problematize their primary partner helped men keep at bay their fear that they were the problem.

Outside partners' willingness to participate in extended sexual encounters functioned as an act of appreciation the men in this study recognized. Scott (40, married) said:

It gives me validation that someone is interested in being with me— sexually and in general since when you're in a relationship for a long time, sometimes the expression of appreciation is lacking a bit, even if they actually do appreciate you.

Scott recognized the probability that his primary partner did appreciate him even though his perception remained that she didn't. Still, his outside partner's willingness to make him feel desired remained important.

Ultimately, these outside partnerships helped them feel better about themselves. Every man in the study mentioned their appreciation and value of their outside partner praising them: their looks, their sexual skills, their penis size. Men especially appreciated outside partners who made some reference to the idea that their primary partners were "really missing out" through their disinterest in them. Thus, outside partnerships provided a space of healing and mending. The experience of their spouses' lack of interest challenged them. Jake (48, married) said:

I seek an outside partner [who] actually wants me, who's turned on by my touch, and desires me. Without the desire and need from the other partner or my spouse, [sex is] a major turn-off. If my partner acts like they are doing me a "favor" by having sex with me, it's pretty much pointless, and I lose the mood.

Jake expressed a common sentiment: we want our partners to want us. We can imagine that sex with a partner who approaches it as a chore or favor wouldn't be satisfying. However, we lack their primary partner's narrative. So, it's impossible to know for certain whether their primary partners truly approach sex as a favor or labor, or whether the men's expectations were unrealistic. But what matters is that the men experience those encounters in that way. Again, the men's perceptions of this as real makes it a de facto reality to them.

They experienced their wife's lack of interest as hurtful, but having outside partners provided reassurance. They also helped men remain in marriages. Holden (41, married) said:

It also provides me with confidence and a fulfilling of my sexual needs. My sense of self-worth is tied quite closely to feelings of being desired. Since my wife shows no desire for me, my [outside] relationships have all made me feel that I am desirable. I feel much more at peace.

Holden voices something fascinating here. We tend to position women as the group whose self-esteem results from being sexually desirable. However, the men in this study made clear that their own sense of self-worth rested on feeling desired. Whatever else we conclude about these men, they shared their feelings bravely and fully. Brock (32, married) explained that approval from women proved important.

I need female attention or I feel incomplete as a person. I always have my whole life. Sought it from my friends (most of my friends have always been women), lovers, coworkers, teachers, really anywhere I could get it. Now I seek it from an [outside partner].

Brock explains that his sense of self is intertwined with attention from women. Again, we tend to believe that this need for validation from the other sex is specific to women. But this sentiment came up repeatedly.

Within outside partnerships, men felt wanted, desired, and accepted. These relationships served their sexual needs, but the boost to their sense of self and their sense of their own masculinity proved the bigger gain. Donald (61, married) shared, "It felt so good to me when not only the sexual act itself was great, but when a woman actually paid some attention to me, and knew exactly how to appeal to my ego or sense of self." Men's narratives reinforced that they highly valued the attention and validation. After years of suffering in silence with feelings of inadequacy and emasculation, men basked in the attention of their outside partners. Their self-confidence benefitted.

The fact that these relationships existed as illicit affairs was not lost on these men. Brock (32, married) added, "It's good to be desired and needed. Especially considering that them having you comes at a great personal risk to themselves." Thus, the fact that outside partnerships required so much effort to maintain and that the detection of them could cost the women everything worked to bolster men's self-esteem. Men internalized their outside partner's willingness to participate in a clandestine affair as an act of prioritizing them and proof of themselves as desirable sexual partners. Being desired felt good. Sloan (36, married) "My outside partner is always excited to see me. They look forward to our time together, which makes me feel valued, attractive, and generally happy." The fact that outside partners willingly risked everything to see the men proved their worth as a sexual partner. Their willingness to risk everything to be with *them* meant more, and men internalized this choice as praise. This also helps understand what initially appears to be the vast differences in reporting between men and women on *Ashley Madison*. Most of the women reported willingness to meet these men solely for the opportunity for sexual pleasure and orgasms (Walker, 2018) because the vast majority of them were doing so in an effort to outsource the sexual aspect of their primary partnerships. Men internalized this willingness to meet as prioritizing of them, which made them feel worthy as a sexual partner. Like the minority of women in that group, the men in this study sought to outsource the emotional aspect of their primary partnerships to an outside partner. While sexual encounters featured heavily in both these accounts, what's valued highest are the ways these interactions made them feel. The bulk of women in the previous study sought to outsource the sexual aspect of their primary partnerships; thus, sexual pleasure functioned as their primary concern. Likewise, the men in this study sought to outsource the emotional aspect, so how they felt functioned as their primary concern, and their own pleasure exists as nearly absent in these narratives. This reflects the narratives of the seven women in my previous book who also sought to outsource the emotional aspect of their primary partnership. So, what may initially look like a gender difference really exists as a difference of priority based on the state of their primary partnerships.

Existing research on the importance of feeling sexually desired focuses on women. However, Sarah Hunter Murray found that nearly 95% of the men in her study reported that feeling sexually desired was "very" or "extremely" important to their sexual experiences (Murray, 2018). However, she found that only 12% of her participants reported that their partner made them feel sexually desired. Additionally, men in her study reported that both enthusiasm toward sex and initiating sex factored into the actions that made them feel sexually desirable, both factors mentioned in the narratives of the men in this study.

Masculinity and Sexual Performance

Men's masculinity is in part built upon heterosexual prowess (Fine, Weis, Addelston, & Marusza, 1997; Flood, Gardiner, Pease, & Pringle, 2007; Halkitis, Green, & Wilton, 2004; Kimmel, Hearn, & Connell, 2005; Thorne, 1993). That is, U.S. culture requires men to amass a list of past sexual partners, and frequently demonstrate both insatiable sexual desire and sexual expertise (Fields et al., 2015; Flood et al., 2007; Halkitis et al., 2004; Pascoe, 2011; Ramírez, 1999). The cultural mandate of masculinity demands that men demonstrate sexual prowess again and again, and rack up high numbers of sexual partners with no "finish line" whereupon society pronounces them "masculine" (Fields et al., 2015; Fine et al., 1997; Flood et al., 2007; Halkitis et al., 2004; Pascoe, 2011).

There exists no moment where men are rewarded with the status of "manly enough." They must constantly perform masculinity to reproduce and reify that status (Kimmel, 2000; Kimmel & Aronson, 2004; Kimmel et al., 2005; Pascoe, 2011). As a result, masculinity exists as a precarious status always in danger of loss.

Entering Marriage Inexperienced

Roughly a third of the men in this study reported a perception that they came into marriage inexperienced. Either they were virgins, only had sex with their wives, or had three partners or less before marrying. (Note: The men in this study perceived having had three or fewer partners as being inexperienced.) At present, the average number of sexual partners in the United States for a man is 7.7 partners (Everett, 2013). Further, the fact that eighteen of these men (39% of the sample) fell into Generation X, touted as the most prolific in terms of sexual partners with a 13.1 lifetime partner count for everyone and 16.1 for Gen X men, likely impacted men's perceptions as well (Duff, 2018). Beyond the actual data, the expectations of masculinity suggest that "real men" rack up high partner counts. Thus, these men may perceive themselves as inexperienced.

This lack of experience with previous partners worked to reinforce their sense of having failed with wives whose orgasms proved absent during marital sex. Kurt (33, married) elaborated:

> I was a late bloomer. Even [in high school] I lacked the self-confidence to ask someone out until I was a junior, and [even then] not much physical beyond basic kissing. I could ask girls out, but DOING anything beyond that was still out of my comfort zone. I graduated high school having never even touched a boob. [At] the age of 22, I proposed to the first woman I ever had sex with. I lost my virginity 2 months shy of my 22nd birthday, and 8 months later was engaged.

For Kurt, his previous reticence to initiate sexual activity with women now plagued him. With his current marital dynamics, where he believed his primary partner to lack interest in sexual activity with him, his youth stood as missed opportunities and foolish choices. He believed his own lack of confidence to have limited his sexual opportunities, resulting in his engagement to his only sexual partner to that date.

For men whose self-confidence dictated a lack of dating experience alongside a lack of sexual experience, unsatisfying marital sexual relationships proved even more challenging. Given their current unsatisfying sexual lives, they often reframed their youth as at best "wasted time," and at worst the cause for their sexual "failures." Kurt elaborated:

> I would like to think that had I been more alpha-male as a youth that I indeed would not be sitting here now typing this to you. I'm looking back on my high school and college days and wondering what the hell was wrong with me. Here I was, 26-27 years old, married, and getting laid so infrequently that the word "annual" was best suited to describe it. All I could think about was all the tail I should have been getting back when I could.

In the face of failed marital sexual lives, sexual inexperience taunted them like lost opportunities. For Kurt, looking back on his dating life proved frustrating. He believed his lack of confidence cost him sexual experiences, and led him to his current situation: a marriage devoid of frequent sexual activity. In his primary partnership, infrequent sexual activity punctuated even their early years together. Kurt correlated this lack of experience with their decision to have an affair. He added:

> The impetus for my affairs is 100% my lack of previous experience magnified by my current lack of frequency. I'd like to think that if I had much more experience, I wouldn't be so curious about what I'm missing. Maybe I'd be more bored with sex. Even if my wife and I were currently enjoying a fantastically healthy sex life, I'd still have that little tickle in the back of my head that I don't REALLY know what's going on.

Kurt recognized on some level that no amount of sexual satisfaction with his primary partner would allay his concerns about having missed out in his youth. So, while he expressed frustration and resentment with his primary partnership's sexual dynamics, some part of him realized that his curiosity would prove irresistible even in the best of circumstances.

Thus, for these men, their histories now served as regrets, and that lack of experience played into their current decision-making.

Other men echoed these sentiments as well. The sense of "having missed out" proved salient for this group of men. Ozzy (41, married) said:

> I met my wife at age 18 and have been with her ever since. I did not cheat until I was 37. I also wanted to have sex with other women to experience it. I had only had sex with my wife (we met when I was 18) and one high school girlfriend, and I wanted a lot more sexual experiences.

Ozzy believed he somehow missed out by practicing monogamy and only having had two previous sexual partners. Interestingly, Ozzy reported only one outside partnership to me: his current one, which had been ongoing for a number of years. The relationship functioned as intense, with both partners exchanging "I love yous" and taking trips together. So, while he says he wanted "a lot more sexual experiences," his participation in outside partnerships amounts to one ongoing, intense, love relationship.

However, other men acted on the feeling of having "missed out" and went on to participate in multiple outside partnerships. Byron (57, married) said:

> I will tell you that I was a virgin until age 21, and I lost that to my future wife whom I had been dating for four years. Even though I was a multi-sport high school and college athlete, I did not consider myself to be all that attractive. Looking back, I probably had many opportunities that I did not recognize at the time.

Byron voices a sense of lost time and regret that he failed to explore sexually in his youth. As they endured on in marriages where sexual activity occurred with partners who viewed sex like a chore and did not experience orgasms, they now saw those youthful decisions as unwise and regretted them. Byron maintains an ongoing outside partnership of two decades, but also participates in other concurrent outside partnerships. His experiences echo many of the women I interviewed in my previous book. Twenty-two of the women reported maintaining multiple outside partnerships concurrent to one another as a means to ensure they never relied on a single partner to fulfill all their needs, as they had done in their primary partnerships (Walker, 2018). In this study, only eight (roughly 17% of the sample) men reported a practice of participation in multiple, concurrent outside partnerships. However, this difference likely exists as a function of the specific aspect of their primary partnerships men sought to outsource to outside partners. Among the women in my last study who also sought to outsource the emotional aspect of their primary partnerships, none reported concurrent outside partnerships.

Despite entering marriage lacking experience, these men committed themselves to becoming great in bed. Byron elaborated, "Although we were both inexperienced, I was totally ready to do whatever it took to have a great sex life and I expected that my wife would want the same. Unfortunately, our views on this subject were not compatible." Men reported conducting extensive research in an effort to self-educate on better sexual techniques in order to function as a worthier sexual partner. Men reported spending hours researching better techniques online and in books and magazines. They were determined to perform masculinity through sexual prowess, and to be a worthy sexual partner to their wives. Patrick (33, married) explained:

> I knew I came into this marriage inexperienced (had only slept with one other woman prior to marriage). I really have tried to study what she likes, ask her, try new things, try to live by the notion that you start making love to her by the way you treat her from the morning till the evening, etc.

Men reported spending a lot of time trying to figure out how to be better in bed. Entering a lifelong union requiring monogamy without prior sexual experience played a role in these men's perceptions of their marital sexual lives as well as their decision to participate in infidelity. Additionally, the lack of experience may well have impacted their decision to enter into a marriage with a partner whose sexual needs, desires, preferences, and interests so differed from their own. For these men, their lack of prior sexual experience only accentuated their distress with their current situation. Looking back, those missed opportunities mocked and taunted their current inability to inspire desire and pleasure in their wives. The result was lives spent in frustration and uncertainty regarding their own sexual prowess, and by extension, their sense of themselves as men. Here again is the need for validation, which sometimes drives men to pursue multiple sexual partners to amass a list of women to provide validation of his prowess (Brooks, 1995; Elder, Brooks, & Morrow, 2012).

Life Is Passing Me By

Experiences with outside partners stood in sharp contrast to their primary partnerships, where men interpreted their primary partners' disinterest in sensual, extended sexual sessions as a rejection of them as desirable. Outside partners expressed sexual desire for the men and preferred long, sensual sessions. The men appreciated this provision. Tripp (48, married) explained:

> It's no longer a "Wham bam, thank you, ma'am." It does add a certain optimism, uplift to the day. You're involved with somebody, who is there pretty much for the same reason. You feel life hasn't completely passed you by.

The men in this study described the sexual validation experienced in outside partnerships as a cure for worry that their lives lacked adequate excitement and sexual opportunities. For some men, these affairs came in the nick of time. Ozzy (41, married) explained:

> For years, I wondered if I would live my life and die being sexually unfulfilled. I now understand what it is to be fully desired and sexually satisfied. I have now been with an attractive younger woman, who desires me completely and is aroused by my appearance.

The sense of concern about life passing them by came up repeatedly. Popular culture even developed a slang term to describe this: FOMO or Fear of Missing Out. For the men in this study, FOMO, a sensation of time running out, and worry that they were settling for less proved salient. Primary partnerships where partners lacked interest in spending hours in bed exacerbated these fears. Outside partners alleviated them through their willingness to engage in extended sessions, which served as validation for men. It's worth noting that it is certainly possible outside partners' willingness was the result of the nature of their association— specifically that the two met in a hotel room, and meetings were both planned in advance and sporadic. Thus, what the men interpreted as interest in them may in fact be a byproduct of the affair dynamic. In my last book, women talked extensively about the need to make the time spent with an outside partner "worth it" because that existed as time taken from other things in their lives (e.g., work, family, chores) (Walker, 2018).

Given the average age of men in this study was 45.9, their reported concerns around "life passing you by" may be related to the popular notion of the "midlife crisis." For many men, the transition into being an "elderly man" is "marked for anxiety and feelings of irrelevance" (Keith, 2017, p. 406). As men age, they often experience "a point in [their] lives when their opinions are not solicited as much… and this decrease in interest in them equates for many to… becoming invisible" (Keith, 2017, p. 406). The men in this inquiry experienced tremendous injury as a result of their perception of their primary partners' loss of interest in them. This injury led them to seek out validation in outside partnerships, which helped them avoid the feeling that "life was passing them by."

Conclusion

Outside partners provided the Girlfriend Experience, characterized by lingering touch, deep kisses, and leisurely encounters (Sanders, 2008). Men interpreted their outside partners' willingness and interest in making time for extended sexual sessions as proof of their desire for them and their approval of the men as sexual partners. Further, men spoke of realizations that their self-esteem came from women's praise and approval. For the men in this study, feeling desired proved important. Outside partners made them feel sexually desirable, experiences that stood in contrast to the dynamics in their primary partnerships, where men reported a belief that their primary partners lacked interest in them. Ultimately, the ways outside partners made men feel proved most valued and salient in their narratives.

Many men reported a lack of sexual experience going into marriage, which allowed the sex in their marriages to serve as their only sense of themselves in terms of prowess. As a result, many men bemoaned their misspent youth, wishing they had spent the time dating more and experiencing other sexual partners. Some men reported their marital sex lives as disappointing from the onset. For others, things waned over time. For all of the men in this study, their outside partnerships functioned to soothe hurt feelings, resentment, and inferiority. Men reported highly valuing having a partner who expressed sexual desire for them, and enthusiasm for sexual activity with them. Further, these outside partnerships helped alleviate FOMO. Concerns of missing out or a sense of life passing them by remained salient.

References

Bachen, C., & Illouz, E. (1995). Imagining romance: Young people's cultural models of romance and love. *Critical Studies in Media Communication, 13*(4), 279–308. https://doi.org/10.1080/15295039609366983.

Brooks, G. R. (1995). *The Jossey-Bass social and behavioral science series: The centerfold syndrome: How men can overcome objectification and achieve intimacy with women.* San Francisco, CA: Jossey-Bass.

Duff, A. (2018). MAGIC NUMBERS The average number of sexual partners for each generation... from baby boomers to millennials: It looks as though generation X are having a whole lot of fun. *The Sun.* Retrieved from https://www.thesun.co.uk/fabulous/7993365/average-number-sexual-partners-generation/.

Elder, W. B., Brooks, G. R., & Morrow, S. (2012). Sexual self-schemas of heterosexual men. *Psychology of Men & Masculinity, 13*(2), 166–179. https://doi.org/10.1037/a0024835.

Everett, B. G. (2013). Sexual orientation disparities in sexually transmitted infections: Examining the intersection between sexual identity and sexual behavior. *Archives of Sexual Behavior, 42*(2), 225–236. https://doi.org/10. 1007/s10508-012-9902-1.

Feasey, R. (2008). *Masculinity and popular television.* Edinburgh: Edinburgh University Press.

Fields, E. L., Bogart, L. M., Smith, K. C., Malebranche, D. J., Ellen, J., & Schuster, M. A. (2015). "I always felt i had to prove my manhood": Homosexuality, masculinity, gender role strain, and HIV risk among young black men who have sex with men. *American Journal of Public Health, 105*(1), 122–131. https://doi.org/10.2105/AJPH.2013.301866.

Fine, M., Weis, L., Addelston, J., & Marusza, J. (1997). (In)secure times: Constructing white working-class masculinities in the late 20th century. *Gender & Society, 11*(1), 52–68. https://doi.org/10.1177/089124397011 001004.

Flood, M., Gardiner, J. K., Pease, B., & Pringle, K. (2007). *International encyclopedia of men and masculinities.* Abingdon, Oxon: Routledge.

Foss, K. A. (2008). "You're gonna make it after all": Changing cultural norms as described in the lyrics of sitcom theme songs, 1970–2001. *Rocky Mountain Communication Review, 4*(2), 43–57.

Gerbner, G., Gross, L., Morgan, M., Signorielli, N., & Shanahan, J. (2002). Growing up with television: Cultivation processes. In J. Bryant & D. Zillmann (Eds.), *LEA's communication series: Media effects: Advances in theory and research* (pp. 43–67). Mahwah, NJ: Lawrence Erlbaum Associates Publishers.

Halkitis, P. N., Green, K. A., & Wilton, L. (2004). Masculinity, body image, and sexual behavior in HIV-seropositive gay men: A two-phase formative behavioral investigation using the Internet. *International Journal of Men's Health, 3*(1), 27–42.

Keith, T. (2017). *Masculinities in contemporary American culture.* New York: Routledge.

Kimmel, M. (2000). *The gendered society.* Oxford: Oxford University Press.

Kimmel, M., & Aronson, A. (2004). *Men and masculinities: A social, cultural, and historical encyclopedia* (Vol. A–J). Santa Barbara: ABC Clio.

Kimmel, M. S., Hearn, J., & Connell, R. W. (2005). *Handbook of studies on men and masculinities.* Thousand Oaks, CA: Sage.

Murray, S. H. (2018). *I want you to want me: Men need to feel sexually desired too.* Paper presented at the Scientific Study of Sexuality (SSSS) Annual Meeting, Montreal, Canada.

Pascoe, C. J. (2011). *Dude, you're a fag masculinity and sexuality in high school, with a new preface.* Berkeley and Los Angeles: University of California Press.

Ramírez, R. L. (1999). *What it means to be a man: Reflections on Puerto Rican masculinity*. New Brunswick, NJ: Rutgers.

Sanders, T. (2008). Male sexual scripts: Intimacy, sexuality and pleasure in the purchase of commercial sex. *Sociology, 42*(3), 400–417. https://doi.org/10.1177/0038038508088833.

Thorne, B. (1993). *Gender play: Girls and boys in school*. New Brunswick, NJ: Rutgers University Press.

Walker, A. M. (2014). Revenge of the beta boys: Opting out as an exercise in masculinity. *McGill Journal of Education, 49*(1), 183–200.

Walker, A. M. (2018). *The secret life of the cheating wife: Power, pragmatism, and pleasure in women's infidelity*. Lanham, MD: Lexington Books.

Wiederman, M. W. (2005). The gendered nature of sexual scripts. *The Family Journal, 13*(4), 496–502. https://doi.org/10.1177/1066480705278729.

7

"Guys Who Suck in Bed Are the Butt of Jokes": The Pressure to Perform

Introduction

The men in this study expressed concern that they might become the "butt" of jokes should partners find their sexual performance lacking. They spoke of keen awareness that men's sexual failures serve as comic fodder in mainstream culture. They mentioned both fictional portrayals and experiences with friends and partners that drove this point home. For these men, the pressure to perform well in bed proved salient. They reported a sense of concern that one bad performance may label them forever. At the same time, men believed that their sexual prowess could compensate for other perceived shortcomings.

The Need for Validation

In Gary Brooks' (1995) book, *The Centerfold Syndrome*, he explained that heterosexual men often develop "highly dysfunctional sexual self-schema based on masculinity socialization," which in turn makes it "difficult for men to establish emotionally intimate relationships and

© The Author(s) 2020
A. M. Walker, *Chasing Masculinity*,
https://doi.org/10.1007/978-3-030-49818-4_7

experience sexually gratifying lives" (Brooks, 1995; Elder, Brooks, & Morrow, 2012, p. 167). Within this framework, Brooks presented a concept he called the Need for Validation, which refers to "men's perception that women have power to validate men as sexual performers" (Brooks, 1995, p. 167; Elder et al., 2012). In men's minds, women accomplish this by saying things such as, "that was great!" or "you're the best I've ever had." According to Brooks, this need for validation increases when men sexually partner with a woman they perceive as attractive. This need for validation leads men to amass high partner counts in an effort to gain the validation of multiple women. Men perceive women as capable of both validating and invalidating them as sexual performers. Thus, men risk much when they engage with a new sexual partner, whom they perceive as holding the power to denounce their sexual skills. By extension, men perceive a woman's rejection of them as desirable sexual partners as an invalidation of them as masculine because masculinity requires sexual prowess. In a 2012 study led by William Elder, all of the study participants "expressed the view that women had the power to validate men's masculine self-worth through sexual attention" (Elder et al., 2012, p. 170). The men in this study echo this same sentiment, as well as the idea that a failure to generate sexual interest from a female partner reflected their lack of masculinity.

"Women Tell Their Friends How Bad You Were"

We live in a culture where masculinity rests partially upon men's sexual performance. Cultural examples of this abound. In the United States, we celebrate men's sexual prowess and denigrate his inability to perform satisfactorily in bed. We can find plenty of evidence of this in television shows, movies, songs, books, magazines, and casual discussions (e.g., *Big Bang Theory, Forgetting Sarah Marshall*, Salt-N-Pepa's "Whatta Man," romance novels, women's magazines, such as *Cosmopolitan* Magazine). Women and men alike view this evidence. The men in this study reported awareness of this cultural narrative around men and their sexual abilities. For example, Brock (32, married) explained that much of his concern around delivering a quality sexual experience stemmed from anxiety that his partners would tell their friends about him and his failures. Brock said, "This sounds weird to say, but I think about *Sex and the City* and the four friends always talking about how bad one man or another was in bed." Brock felt the need to preface his concern as "weird," but television shows do provide us with scripts and models to guide us in our real lives, including our romantic lives (Bachen & Illouz, 1995; Gerbner, Gross, Morgan, Signorielli, & Shanahan, 2002). For heterosexual men, watching *SATC* may feel like a rare glimpse into the forbidden world of female friendship and conversation. For Brock—and perhaps for many other men—the show sparked an awareness—or perhaps a confirmation of their fears—that sex with a female partner renders him vulnerable to critique from both her and her friends—because she likely told her friends all about it.

For those unfamiliar with the show, there was much discussion regarding men's sexual prowess or lack thereof. The women dished their partners' ability, penis size, enthusiasm, and acumen. They deemed no detail too graphic for consumption by their friends. A quick *Google* search will deliver a *Revelist* article titled "36 men Samantha Jones fucked on *Sex and the City*–ranked from forgettable to phenomenal. Oh, and one woman," which discusses and grades the characters' sexual perfor- mance. Stop and consider for a moment that a market exists for rankings of the fictional sexual partners of a fictional character. What does that say about how we respond to details of flesh and blood partners—our own and those of our close confidants?

And let's not forget Carrie Bradshaw's one-time experience with Howie Halberstein, a groomsman at Charlotte and Harry's wedding, who jack-rabbited her into a neck cramp that kept her bent over the next day—including her time spent at the wedding—and yet she never tells him she isn't enjoying herself. In fact, when she declines to see him again before he leaves town, Howie is still so convinced that he did a great job in bed, he accuses Carrie of "using [him] for sex," an accusation he rails in front of wedding guests. To the viewer, who knows Howie is terrible in bed, he looks ridiculous, foolish, and clueless. But in reality, Howie is working off the information available to him. During their sexual encounter, Carrie fails to voice her pain, and instead allows him to pound away as she lies there in discomfort. For men with previous female sexual partners who watch this episode, it would be easy to begin reviewing past sexual performances and wondering which women simply suffered in silence, ended the relationship with an excuse, and then complained to all of her friends about how you utterly lack sexual prowess.

Brock's experiences with women evaluating men's performance and discussing it with their friends aren't limited to television shows. He adds:

> Also, something personal to me is that I have always had many close female friends and they would tell me what they didn't like about sex with their various boyfriends/husbands/etc. For me, that has a lot to do with it, too.

Brock's real-life experiences planted the fear that he too may be the butt of his female partners' stories. Watching *Sex and the City* likely solidified the notion that this tendency to dish the details of their sex lives isn't unique to his friends. Many men conclude that while women may not necessarily tell their partner how dissatisfied they were with the performance, they may report their feelings—and perhaps in graphic detail—back to their friends. For men, this exists as a sobering realization. While a 2015 study found that women tend *not* to discuss sex with their friends unless they construct a means to feminize the discussion (Montemurro, Bartasavich, & Wintermute, 2015), other studies found that women discuss sex with their friends more often than men (Lefkowitz, Boone, & Shearer, 2002). In fact, a 2018 study found women discussing sex with their friends correlates with higher sexual self-efficacy and sexual self-esteem. Clearly some women share sexual exploits with friends, and some don't. However, in this study the men's belief that the possibility existed for female partners to tattle to their friends functioned as both anxiety-inducing and motivation to perform at higher levels.

Like many men in this study, Brock's takeaway from this realization was to up his game. Despite referencing the tendency of women to complain about men's sexual performance behind their backs, he still doesn't believe that influences his behavior. He adds, "I get off on it. I don't really feel like it comes from a negative or fear-based place.

I think it really has to do with making me feel good for making others feel good." He frames his behavior as a personality trait rather than a response to social conditioning and social narratives, despite his own acknowledgement of his fear of being the butt of women's sexual gossip.

Brock was not alone in his concerns. Men experienced this pressure to perform as so ubiquitous they assumed everyone felt it. Barry (37, married) said:

> I do feel a ton of pressure to be great at sex. As a man we all want to be like they are in the movies, both porn movies and regular mainstream movies. It comes from the locker room and guys talking about their latest conquests. It comes from expectations to make sure your partner is satisfied and taken care of. I think everyone, in some way, feels that they need to be great at sex.

Notice that Barry framed this desire as originating from discussions of sex among men, rather than women's tendency to discuss their sexual encounters with friends. Regardless of where men pinned the origin, they reported that an awareness of social expectations drove their behavior. Perry (27, married) said, "I succumbed to the female pleasure. That is my goal and all I strive for because of the social media stating that guys aren't doing their jobs." No one wants to end up an internet meme or "that guy" in a woman's bad sex story. Fear of being deemed a guy who "doesn't get the job done" loomed large for men. Brock (32, married) added, "I do feel pressure to be a stud." Being regarded as "great at sex" offered protection from the emasculation of someone reporting your sexual performance as subpar.

Men's fears have some basis. A 2002 study led by Eva S. Lefkowitz found that college-aged women reported a higher frequency of conversations with best friends about sex than men did (Lefkowitz et al., 2002). Dr. Lefkowitz explained that women not only discussed sex more, they were more comfortable with sex-related discussions. She went on to say, "These findings suggest that when men and women get into a relationship, they come from different sexual communication experiences on two levels—frequency and comfort. This mismatch may explain some of the differences and problems that other researchers have identified in marital communication" (State, 2002). In 2015, Sara Levine reported in *Bustle* that a *Reddit* survey came to similar conclusions (Levine, 2015). Thus, evidence exists to suggest that many women tell their friends about their sexual experiences in detail.

"TV Presents Us as Moronic Walking Penises"

Many men I spoke with acknowledged an awareness of common media presentations about men's sexuality, sexual performance, and bodies, and went on to talk about the toll those have. Patrick (33, married) described his experience: "Men are bombarded with [concerns about] physical deficiency, [like] penis not large enough, doesn't last long enough, isn't muscular enough, as well as actions, the right clothes, and probably the biggest: doesn't make enough money to be attractive to a woman." Many men in this study spoke about these heightened expectations of men as potential romantic partners. They also reported that the pressure on men isn't limited to media presentations geared toward women. Patrick went on to add:

> Perhaps you should read and pay attention to men's magazines and see their articles about "erectile dysfunction" and "pre-mature ejaculation" and "Is she dissatisfied with how short you are and [how short you] last." Not to mention the huge bins of "make your penis bigger" moronic herbal crap that adorn every single gas station counter in this country.

Patrick pointed out that these mandates are everywhere. Just as women's magazines press women to live up to impossible standards, men's magazines capitalize on the social pressure on men to be everything women want. Thus, men felt these messages coming from all directions. The pressure to perform well sexually proved salient.

Other men echoed this awareness. Rudy (42, married) explained, "I have noticed discussions in [the] media about guys who suck in bed being the butt of jokes and/or negative comments. Size of their cock, being an octopus, smelling bad, lasting only a few seconds." Men reported penis size features prominently in these media presentations of what men should be. Thus, the men in this study reported concerns around women's acceptance of and desire for them. After all, much of the mandates of masculinity regard physical traits over which men lack control (e.g., penis size, physical size overall). Research shows men internalize media messages and subsequently experience dissatisfaction with body image (Barlett, Vowels, & Saucier, 2008; Grogan, 2016; Hobza, Walker, Yakushko, & Peugh, 2007; Stratton, Donovan, Bramwell, & Loxton, 2015). Concerns with musculature, size, and attractiveness feature prominently. Men internalize media messages commanding them to demonstrate virility and prowess, which includes a larger penis size (Katz, 2002). The men in this inquiry reported an impact from these messages as well.

How do men respond to this pressure? How do they function in a society that ridicules men who don't live up to the standard? They try to be so good in bed no one has cause for complaint. Rudy said:

> I can say that in the back of my mind [was the thought that] I didn't want to be "that guy," which is why I always strived to make sure my partners had an orgasm, or got to the point where they just wanted me in them.

While concern for your partner's pleasure is desirable, for these men, the pressure to provide their partner's pleasure stems from a desire to demonstrate their masculinity. The focus on her orgasm focuses less on her experience and more on how it validates men's prowess. While it may be easy to fault the men in this study for their framing of their sexual encounters, it's important to remember that they're responding to cultural and social expectations. Deciding that this is simply a group of "bad apples" ignores the very structures in place creating the anxiety men feel that leads them to *need* their partners to orgasm as confirmation of their masculinity via sexual skill.

These men both acknowledged and resented these messages. Patrick (33, married) explained, "I believe most men feel pressure that their sexual performance is somehow substandard. [It's] a stereotype in modern media that is problematic sexually. If you watched some TV shows, you'd think men were just these moronic walking penises." Many men acknowledged the sense that the prevailing stereotypes of men include "bad in bed." Should you doubt this, do a quick *Google* search for memes about men being bad in bed. You'll quickly see examples of this ranging from film stills with movie quotes punctuating the joke (e.g., Matthew McConaughey from *The Wolf of Wall Street* with his character's line, "You've gotta get those numbers up. Those are rookie numbers" in reference to men's stamina), to reality television stars (e.g., Snookie pictured drinking a margarita with the tagline: "Wanna know the difference between a man and a margarita? A margarita hits the spot every time") to text-only relationship proclamations centering upon the value of "good sex" (e.g., "Life is too short for bad sex"). These men begrudged the ways media messages reduced them and their value to their sexual performance. After all, we rarely see media representations presenting women as bad in bed, nor do we see presentations suggesting her skills in bed determine her femininity. The men explained that these presentations resulted in damaging internalized narratives. Sloan (36, married) added:

> Just like [the] media objectifies women, it portrays men as perpetually aroused, always looking to show off his sexual prowess, with "real men" always bringing women to orgasmic bliss. Guys in the media who can't get or please a woman are always portrayed as dorky and undesirable. Any boy growing up is going to want to be desirable, and therefore the media tells him he has to be great at sex.

Men experienced these media messages from multiple sources. While they attempted to shake off the demands of those social scripts, they found it impossible to completely avoid internalizing them. As a result, they internalized the importance of their sexual skill in validating their masculinity.

Pressure to Perform

Perhaps predictably, twenty-seven (almost 59%) of the men in this study explicitly reported feeling pressure to perform sexually. In the United States, sexual scripts command men to act as initiators of sexual events, demonstrate sexual prowess through provoking women's orgasm, to push their relationships toward physical intimacy, and to experience high levels of sexual desire (Wiederman, 2005). The men in this study lack immunity to our cultural narratives around men's sexuality. They spoke of pressure to be "good in bed," to be the "best" their outside partners had ever had. This pressure to perform existed within their primary partnerships as well. Kurt (33, married) explained, "I think that my need to please has made sex with my wife worse. Because we have sex so infrequently, on the rare occasions that she is in the mood I REALLY feel the need to perform." For these men, primary partners' lack of interest in frequent sex only bolsters their fears that they lack adequate sexual skills. Their need to provoke sexual desire within their primary partners—as proof of their own worth as a sexual partner—placed tremendous stress on those relationships. Holden (41, married) said, "This pressure greatly impacts how I see sex with my wife. The pressure is palpable." Under this burden, the sexual dynamics in their primary partnerships took on extra weight. Often the resulting circumstance was a self-feeding cycle that failed to serve either party. Kurt (33, married) elaborated that when his wife finally consented to sex, the pressure created negative experiences.

> I feel like I've got 2 months' worth of getting it on to get on, and the result is usually that I end up disappointed. I tend to not, ahem, last very long when it's been a dozen weeks or more since my last time, so I know that she's not getting much out of it. The other option is that I do have some longevity, but then I overdo it. Like I said, trying to work 2 months of sex into this one experience. It's kind of a vicious cycle.

We can see in these descriptions that the marital bed functioned as a proving ground, and that pressure led to encounters lacking the pleasure and stress-relief both parties desire. As a result, primary partners may become more disinterested in future encounters. Men experienced these primary partner encounters as further evidence of their inadequacy as lovers, and by extension, as men. Ultimately, this pressure combined with their spouse's disinterest challenged the relationship.

The Pressure Is Only on Men

Men in this study felt their wives failed to experience comparable pressure to perform. Patrick (33, married) said, "I felt pressure to provide a pleasurable sexual experience for her; I assumed that I was an inexperienced lover, so I studied and put lots of effort into knowing what I needed to know, etc." Many men spoke of working very hard to provide a quality experience for their wives. However, their wives refused to act in kind, which served to generate resentment within the men. Patrick (33, married) elaborated, "Yet my wife was educated by the same magazine/TV society that just a 'warm body in a bed' was all a man wanted." Many men took offense at what they perceived as their primary partner's lack of concern for their sexual pleasure. Men talked about careful research to improve their performance, yet noted that their wives failed to engage in similar work. The men experienced this as unfair and unbalanced. Men grew resentful and bitter in response to their perception of this unbalanced pressure to perform.

Beyond their spouses' lack of concern with their own sexual performance, they seemed indifferent about keeping their husbands' interest. Patrick (33, married) explained that his wife found that "the expectation to stay fit and attractive was chauvinistic and unrealistic. She has refused to make sex and attractiveness important in our relationship." (Only two men mentioned their wives' weight.) For Patrick, his primary partner's disinterest in keeping his sexual interest as an object of his desire flew in the face of his own steady work toward coming into the bedroom as a skilled partner. He believed that given the level of work he put into readying himself to be a worthy partner, his primary partner's utter apathy about whether he found her attractive read as "entitled." His indignation at her entitlement to his sexual prowess while doing nothing whatsoever to contribute to a pleasing sexual experience for him ate at him. While the men I spoke to expressed concern about providing a quality sexual experience for their partners, they struggled with wives who lacked the same investment. Patrick (33, married) clarified, "I'm not saying ultra-spicy… just important to her." This harkens back to men's desires for their primary partners to just *like* them. Men framed their expectations as quite low.

Many men wanted to be sure that I understood their expectations were not unreasonable. Men interpreted their perception of women's lack of "preparation" for sex and low level of energy expended as offensive and dismissive because they were engaging in high levels of both. Although they remained aware of cultural mandates for men to do so, they still somehow assumed women felt a similar need or pressure to do so, and experienced their partner's failure to do as rejection. They spoke of disappointment that their primary partners failed to also invest in the creation/maintenance of satisfying sexual experiences in the marriage, but immediately worried that I would deem their concerns excessive. In fact, they quantified all of their concerns regarding sex with the worry that I would find them trivial or unreasonable. There existed a clear sense that society failed to value their feelings regarding this topic.

Further, men experienced as novel their outside partner's tendency to not only express sexual desire, but to take responsibility for their own orgasms and offer clear guidance. Their frustration with their primary partner's unwillingness to offer guidance or demonstrate desire echoes previous research which found that both men and women perceive part of women's sexual responsibility as being psychologically prepared to orgasm (Salisbury & Fisher, 2014). Thus, the irritation these men feel with their primary partner's lack of preparation for sexual activity may stem from their deeper perception that their partners failed to psychologically ready themselves to experience orgasm.

"She's Not Holding Up Her End"

The men in this study experienced this disparity as hurtful and indicative of a lack of concern and affection for them, and they resented the one-way focus in their marriages. Sloan (36, married) explained:

> I think it's interesting how many magazines and talk shows dedicate time to how men need to be more romantic and appreciative of their partner, but nothing about why it is also important for women to take time to make their men feel sexually desirable. Most men I know could use help with romance, but that doesn't mean women shouldn't be working on the sexual side of things too.

Men spoke of the expectations of themselves as lovers, but also the frustration that women aren't similarly socialized to bear some responsibility as well. When I mentioned the tendency of women's magazines to demand women "spice up" their sex lives and learn "moves to make [their] man crazy in bed," men dismissed those as not mainstream or prevalent enough to parallel their own experiences. Perhaps they're correct. Women's magazines tend to frame the payoff of "spicing things up" as enhanced pleasure for themselves as well.

The painful nature of their sexual lives—or lack thereof—with their wives was palpable in these narratives. The men saw the state of their sexual relationships with their wives as their own personal failure. Sloan (36, married) said:

> The pressure to be good at sex makes me feel responsible for figuring everything out in the bedroom with my wife. She's not a very sexually-driven woman. Because I want to have sex regularly, I felt like it was/is my responsibility to figure out exactly what she'll enjoy the most. I have to introduce any new moves, positions, fantasies, etc.

Once again, we see the narrative of men's hard work to perform sexual prowess and producing orgasms, and their wives not responding in kind. Unsurprisingly, many men felt resentful as a result. Sloan articulated this:

> As I think about this, I find myself annoyed that I am responsible for her figuring out her turn-ons. It would be a lot easier if she knew what she liked and went after it, instead of me hoping she'll be excited by something I introduce.

Men expressed frustration with primary partners whom they perceived left the responsibility for their own orgasms to the men, and provided no feedback or guidance as to how to provoke that. By contrast, men described outside partners' commitment to their own pleasure, and as providing guidance and feedback to show the way to the provocation of orgasm. Primary partners who felt no responsibility for their own pleasure and/or had no real interest in pleasure—at least with them—represented failure and frustration for the men. The men took on the responsibility for providing sexual pleasure to their wives; that responsibility weighed heavily; men grew bitter as a result.

You're Only as Good as Your Last Performance

While outside partnerships existed as spaces of soothing and healing from the emotional hurt sustained in their primary partnerships, these encounters also served as sources of pressure. After all, both parties still exist within U.S. culture where a man demonstrates masculinity through sexual prowess. That narrative manifests itself as pressure to perform well the first meeting—or risk never having another opportunity to prove themselves. Milo (29, married) explained:

> I'm not sure where the pressure comes from really, but in my mind, I feel that if I don't perform the first time that there won't be a second. ha-ha. Sort of like, a first impression or first date. It's like all these girls are expecting great sex FROM us. All we expect from you is to show up and be willing (we're lucky to even get that); now if you show up and participate, that's just a huge bonus. ha-ha.

Here, the men's data echoes the findings of my previous study on women on this topic. The majority of the women with whom I spoke stated plainly that since their entire motivation was orgasms, they quickly cast aside any man who failed to induce them. Women spoke of requiring men to "bring their A game each and every time" they met for sex, and that if a man failed to do so he'd be replaced (Walker, 2018). The men in this study reported an awareness of that reality. Many men felt that each "first time" with a new partner was an audition where a bad showing resulted in "being cut" early—and the women's data confirms that is typically the case (Walker, 2018). Women spoke of feeling they were in control of outside partnerships. Some men in this study echoed that sentiment. Byron (57, married) said:

> I have come to the conclusion that *AM* [*Ashley Madison*] (and probably other sites as well) is a site that is designed for women much more than men. The women get to make the decisions as to whom they want to meet. The men send messages, requests, or opportunities, but the women get to pore through them and pick what they want to pursue. Usually no response is received even acknowledging a message.

Thus, the dynamics of outside partnerships replicated some of the power-lessness men described within their primary partnerships. Men perceived women as choosing to initiate sexual relationships with them, and choosing whether to continue within those. Meanwhile, they believed they competed with scads of other men on *Ashley Madison.*

This perception heightened the pressure attached to an initial meeting with a new outside partner. Men felt a stellar performance necessary. Scott (40, married) said:

> So, when meeting a [partner] for the first time, there are all these variables that make it somewhat hard to relax and just have a good time. Couple that with me just NOT being an uncontrollable hormone machine, it takes a bit more mental stimulation to get me going.

Men realized they labored under unrealistic expectations, yet still felt pressure to meet them. The pressure men endured in outside partner-ships stemmed from concerns about performance, size, and ability to provoke orgasm. Each man operated as though he could be cut out of his lover's life at any moment. And the reality was that he could be.

Given the fact that both men and women I spoke with believed that men outnumber women on *Ashley Madison*, women do enjoy some power and control over the formation and maintenance of these relation-ships. As a result, women report an unwillingness to maintain outside partnerships where the sex is bad, and men report pressure to perform well from the first meeting forward. Women explain that given what they're risking by having an affair, and given that they're seeking a partner due to bad sex at home or a sexless marriage, they're unwilling to endure bad sex in an outside partnership. For them, their practices stem from pragmatism. However, for men the unfamiliarity of a new partner can directly impact the quality of an initial sexual encounter. Scott explained:

If [it] was an ongoing thing, I think it becomes a bit easier after a while. It's easier to be more comfortable as you get to know the person better. Things like performance issues are easier to deal with in other ways. But when the [outside partner] is someone you just met or you're only a date or two into the relationship, there's no pattern established to say "this is just a temporary issue." You're still establishing the pattern of your relationship with the OP [outside partner]. At an old job I had, when we'd have an initial success, it was dubbed "one in a row," as a joke and a reminder that you can't establish direction or pattern based on one occurrence. But if you meet up with an [outside partner] and the first, second, and third times don't go so well, you've established a pattern, and it's likely you're not going to get many more "dates." So, there's some anxiety there too.

Both men and women reported an awareness that first sexual encounters between sexual partners are often unsatisfying, and that sex tends to get better over time with familiarity. Regardless, the circumstances remained. Women in my study reported that a particularly bad first sexual encounter typically meant they wouldn't see the man again.

Some men responded to this expectation with a determination to "up their game" each time. Marcello (44, married) explained:

With my lover, my whole goal is for them to be a little bit more turned on about me by the time I leave. To try different things. To eat her in a new angle: on the windowsill, in the shower or in the mirror room (yes, she has a mirror room). It has made me a better pussy-eater. I had this lover when I was 21 [who] was 30. She worked me over till I got it perfect FOR HER and then I adjusted with each lady. [It's] my saving grace.

Many men spoke of efforts to continuously bring their top performance, to surprise their partner, to learn as much as possible about how to deliver quality sexual pleasure to their partner. Despite all that research and focus, anxieties remained. Marcello explained that regardless of his expertise at cunnilingus and his commitment to providing novelty, he still feels pressure to "have hour-long sex sessions with my cock inside. It's like I should have trained well enough by doing exercises to hold it that long." Marcello expresses a sense that regardless of how many orgasms he delivers to his outside partner, no number exists as "enough." Further, regardless of prowess at oral sex, men felt pressure to deliver using their penis as well.

For many men, this is especially a concern if they are very turned on by a woman, or if their interest in her is especially high. Marcello elaborated, "The truth is if I REALLY LIKE the gal, she is real trouble in that department because I just climax all over right off the bat. The good thing is that I'm also into round two." Consistently bringing their best performance and investigating new ways to please served as common strategies to combat this pressure among this group. However, anxieties still came to bear. Scott (40, married) explained, "I think the worst pressure I get—and maybe other men—is just lasting long enough to satisfy [my] partner. The pressure I put on myself just involves being in the mood when I'm supposed to be. Ha-ha." The mandate of modern masculinity in the United States includes men being perpetually "ready" to have sex. The reality differs significantly. Men struggle with being "in the mood" just as women do. Scott explained that the very nature and structure of outside partnerships creates pressure. He explained:

> I know that sounds odd, but when I can only meet my current [outside partner] once every two weeks or so, and usually longer than that, I don't want to disappoint. The stress and worry of getting caught, dealing with the needs and personalities of people you're trying to establish an outside relationship with, and, of course, for men, the stress and such can contribute to "performance anxiety."

The stress of getting naked with a new partner, ensuring an adequate alibi, concern about seeing someone you know in a place where you can't easily explain your presence, and even guilt over cheating all come into play when two outside partners met for sex. Any one of those things alone could prevent an erection. Imagine them in combination. Still, Scott felt confident some men weren't impacted. He elaborated:

I'm sure some guys are ready to go as long as there's a willing partner who meets their standards for "attractive." But for me—and I'm sure other guys—distractions, stress, mood, etc. Lots of stuff can cause us not to perform very well. To be blunt, as easy as it seems to be for guys to get erections, it's fairly easy to prevent them as well.

While he understood the reality of his own capacity, he assumed other men (perhaps more masculine men) possessed greater capabilities. In media presentations, failure to achieve erections sets up men for ridicule (e.g., *The Office* did an entire episode about it). An inability to produce an erection on command—and for as long as is "needed" or wanted—positions men to be shamed, mocked, and to have their masculinity questioned.

Thus, the men perceived women as in control of the outside partnership arena. Interestingly, in *The Secret Life of the Cheating Wife*, women believed that as well (Walker, 2018). After all, the men perceived themselves as desperate for a partner, for praise, for opportunities to demonstrate their virility. Women controlled those opportunities. Travis (43, married) explained:

> For a guy, he wants to satisfy his partner so that she'll want more. I think a woman is always in control of the relationship moving forwards at this point. If she's satisfied, she'll want more and the relationship will continue, maybe flourish. If she's not, well, he has to have some redeeming factor that tells her he's worth keeping or it goes no further.

Thus, successful, ongoing outside partnerships functioned as healing. However, the formation of new outside partnerships proved stressful and anxiety-producing. After all, their female partners gatekept access to the relationship. If the women failed to experience adequate pleasure to deem the association "worth it," the men's opportunities ended. Thus, for the men, they perceived women as controlling all sexual access in their lives: their wives at home, and their outside partners in their affairs. If they fail to live up to the expectations, they're locked out.

Strategies and Compensations

In response to the pressure to perform and in an effort to avoid the stigma—real or imagined—of underperforming, some men developed compensation strategies. Remember, men often engage in acts of compensatory masculinity when they perceive a threat to their masculinity. In this case, the men's belief that a failure to deliver the "best sex ever" functioned as a threat to their sense of themselves as masculine. Donald (61, married) said:

> That pressure to become a great lover—or at the very least an adequate lover (minimally acceptable or attaining standard performance)—forced me to become very skilled at cunnilingus and other kinds of extended foreplay as well as delaying ejaculation. Another reason my friend became interested in me was because I had openly advertised on the *AM* [*Ashley Madison*] site that I love performing cunnilingus. That appealed to her very much.

Oral sex served as a way to delineate themselves from other contenders. Many men proudly reported their predilection for and skill in providing oral sex to their sexual partners. Furthermore, many men reported this with a belief that it separated them from most other men. Gus (62, married) described his experience: "I know research has shown that >80% of women are unable to achieve orgasm through intercourse and require clitoral stimulation to get off. I focus on providing the best oral performance I can along with masturbating them." Men spent time researching sex and women's bodies—to the point of proudly quoting statistics to a researcher well-versed in them, no less—and then honed skills to address women's pleasure. In fact, many men opened our interview dialogue with some version of "I'm excited to be interviewed by a real, live sex researcher. But you should know that I'm a sex researcher myself with X years of experience." Many believed themselves experts in the field. While all of this newfound knowledge and application of new techniques is a great thing for their partners, we must see it for what it is: a strategy to improve their chances at seeing an outside partner again, and a mechanism for performing masculinity through sexual prowess.

While it may be easy for us to sit back and judge men for thinking about sex in this way—or even dismiss their concerns—the reality is that our culture promotes the idea that "real men" deliver in the bedroom. Men feared women's critique of their performance—either spoken to his face or behind his back to their friends. No man wanted to be the guy who couldn't make his partner orgasm. Greg (53, married) said:

> Personally, my goal is to bring my partner to orgasm, at least once, prefer-ably multiple, then focus on myself, if needed. If my partner is having fun, I KNOW I am going to have fun. Where does it come from? Our society and the perception that all men are stallions.

Sex functioned as a performance of masculinity in order to gain valida-tion from women. Avoiding stigma motivated much of their behavior, but their reward remained the possibility of praise. Men made the connection: bringing women to orgasm results in praise. For these men, praise proved important. The idea of being humiliated remained salient for men. Because masculinity demands sexual prowess, men perceive women as ultimately holding the power to validate—or invalidate—men's masculinity through their judgment of their sexual performance during any given sexual event. Thus, any time a man chooses to couple with a new partner, he risks his sense of masculinity. As a result, the importance of praise from the female partners in their lives cannot be understated.

Given all the pressure to perform masculinity through sexual prowess, some men described their sexual prowess as a source of confidence. Specifically, they spoke of the ways being talented in bed helped them overcome other shortcomings—real or perceived. For example, men who believed themselves to be less than conventionally attractive could make up for that in the bedroom. Riley (39, married) explained:

> I do put a lot of pressure on myself to be amazing in bed. I've been overweight most of my life, so it comes from that insecurity. I have to be such a good lover that they overlook any other deficits. I know I'm not the most good-looking guy. I've carried extra weight most of my life. I'm not a trendy dresser. I'm not a hugely social person.

For these men, the ability to bring sexual pleasure to a sexual partner countered other perceived deficits. In their minds, whatever flaws they may possess, their sexual skill mitigated them. Holden (41, married) explained, "Look at me: I'm hideous, but Don Juan and Casanova would envy my prowess.;) And, of course, I'm joking about the hideous part. I'm better at sex than most people." For some men, their overall confidence rooted in their sexual skill. Holden (41, married) went on:

> I would say that my sense of confidence has a basis in my sexual prowess. My self-concept is based largely on how well I please others, both sexually and otherwise. I grew up with a very critical father, who I was always trying to please.

Thus, sexual prowess could serve as compensation for other shortcomings, and as a means to gain confidence in other arenas. Confidence in their sexual prowess provided a basis for better general self-esteem. Thus, their sexual performance functioned as a compensatory masculinity strategy. Men felt emasculated by primary partners who either failed to orgasm or lacked interest in the men as lovers. Men described primary partnership dynamics where their wives "couldn't be pleased," and where they constantly disappointed. Thus, outside partnerships exist as another arena where they can demonstrate masculinity and redeem themselves.

These men repeatedly espoused a cultural narrative that men's responsibilities include sexual prowess. Jake (48, married) elaborated:

> I guess the fear that we all feel is that we are a disappointment. I always strive to be my best in the bedroom. There is a desire in me to want to send you to that edge of ecstasy that you have never been to. Now, I'm naive to think that I'll send you over the edge every time, but I'm sure going to try. I guess a man's main concern is that we make sure that our partner orgasms, are we going to me endowed enough... Overall, I guess we want to meet y'all's expectations.

Men drew from scripts regarding "what women want" and tried to measure up to those scripts, which sometimes provide competing narratives. Thus, measuring up literally and figuratively occupied much of men's thoughts. Rudy (42, married) said:

> So, the pressure is again on me to perform. I don't try to outdo my last performance each time, but I do like to keep repeat meetings with partners interesting and a little different [from] the last time. Focus on what I learned she liked and try new things to see what happens. As I met other women, I learned more details about what they liked to see in guys that they hooked up with, whether that be for short-term or long-term relationships. I didn't want to be a guy talked about negatively, so I focused on developing the traits that these ladies liked.

Men researched effective sexual strategies, but they also studied their partners for clues as to what worked and what didn't. Rudy went on to clarify:

> I've been thinking if the pressure to not be "THAT guy" has significantly impacted me. I wanted to make sure my partners were satisfied, which is why I focused on making sure they had an orgasm before I did.

Indeed, the avoidance of being "that guy" proved salient in the narratives presented here. Men reported keen awareness of their vulnerability to women's critical feedback—either directly to them or behind their backs—and sought to avoid that experience. Given they were functioning in marriages where their wives clearly communicated displeasure with their sexual performance—at least through her disinterest—earning the positive feedback of their outside partners took on heightened importance.

Conclusion

Men spoke of a keen awareness of U.S. cultural ideals around men and sexual performance. Men in this study expressed knowledge that poor sexual performance opened them to ridicule and shame. The concern that one bad encounter may label them permanently—at least in that partner's mind—loomed large. The men deeply wanted every partner they ever had to think positively of their prowess. Men spent time researching strategies and techniques to improve upon their skill. Men who failed to deliver a quality sexual performance on command from the first meeting forward faced consequences: an inability to see the woman again. First impressions served as an all-or-nothing audition. However, once established, men could still lose an ongoing outside partner if they failed to consistently perform. Thus, they experienced a pronounced pressure to perform sexually. On the flip side, they believed that their skill and ability in bed compensated for other areas where they fall short.

References

Bachen, C., & Illouz, E. (1995). Imagining romance: Young people's cultural models of romance and love. *Critical Studies in Media Communication, 13*(4), 279–308. https://doi.org/10.1080/15295039609366983.

Barlett, C. P., Vowels, C. L., & Saucier, D. A. (2008). Meta-aanalyses of the effects of media images on men's body-image concerns. *Journal of Social and Clinical Psychology, 27*(3), 279–310.

Brooks, G. R. (1995). *The Jossey-Bass social and behavioral science series. The centerfold syndrome: How men can overcome objectification and achieve intimacy with women.* San Francisco, CA: Jossey-Bass.

Elder, W. B., Brooks, G. R., & Morrow, S. (2012). Sexual self-schemas of heterosexual men. *Psychology of Men & Masculinity, 13*(2), 166–179. https://doi.org/10.1037/a0024835.

Gerbner, G., Gross, L., Morgan, M., Signorielli, N., & Shanahan, J. (2002). Growing up with television: Cultivation processes. In J. Bryant & D. Zillmann (Eds.), *LEA's communication series. Media effects: Advances in theory and research* (pp. 43–67). Mahwah, NJ: Lawrence Erlbaum Associates Publishers.

Grogan, S. (2016). *Body image: Understanding body dissatisfaction in men, women and children.* London: Routledge.

Hobza, C. L., Walker, K. E., Yakushko, O., & Peugh, J. (2007). What about men? Social comparison and the effects of media images on body and self-esteem. *Psychology of Men & Masculinity, 8*(3), 161–172. https://doi.org/10.1037/1524-9220.8.3.161.

Katz, J. (2002). Advertising and the construction of violent white masculinity: From eminem to clinique for men. In G. Dines & J. M. Humez (Eds.), *Gender, race, and class in media.* Los Angeles: Sage.

Lefkowitz, E. S., Boone, T. L., & Shearer, C. L. (2002). Communication with best friends about sex-related topics during emerging adulthood. *Journal of Youth and Adolescence, 33*(4), 339–351. https://doi.org/10.1023/B:JOYO.0000032642.27242.c1.

Levine, S. (2015). Guys reveal how much they tell their friends after sex, and it's probably not what you expect. *Bustle.*

Montemurro, B., Bartasavich, J., & Wintermute, L. (2015). Let's (not) talk about sex: The gender of sexual discourse. *Sexuality and Culture, 19*(1), 139–156. https://doi.org/10.1007/s12119-014-9250-5.

Salisbury, C. M. A., & Fisher, W. A. (2014). "Did you come?" A qualitative exploration of gender differences in beliefs, experiences, and concerns regarding female orgasm occurrence during heterosexual sexual interactions. *The Journal of Sex Research, 51*(6), 616–631. https://doi.org/10.1080/00224499.2013.838934.

State, P. (2002). *Women talk about sex more than men do* [Press release]. Retrieved from https://www.eurekalert.org/pub_releases/2002-04/ps-wta041202.php.

Stratton, R., Donovan, C., Bramwell, S., & Loxton, N. J. (2015). Don't stop till you get enough: Factors driving men towards muscularity. *Body Image, 15,* 72–80. https://doi.org/10.1016/j.bodyim.2015.07.002.

Walker, A. M. (2018). *The secret life of the cheating wife: Power, pragmatism, and pleasure in women's infidelity.* Lanham, MD: Lexington Books.

Wiederman, M. W. (2005). The gendered nature of sexual scripts. *The Family Journal, 13*(4), 496–502. https://doi.org/10.1177/1066480705278729.

8

"It's My Job to Make Her Orgasm": Women's Orgasm Provision as Responsibility and Special Skill

Introduction

The men in this study reported a sense of duty with regard to women's orgasms. Specifically, they believed that the provision of orgasms for their partner served as both an achievement and a responsibility. Men reported a sense of themselves as uniquely gifted and skilled in their ability to elicit orgasm, and as such believed they owed a responsibility. Thus, they reported taking pleasure in providing pleasure. However, men's own sexual pleasure remained absent in these narratives. This stands in direct contrast to women's narratives of infidelity (Walker, 2014a, 2014b, 2018), where the bulk of the women focused on their own sexual gratification. Ultimately, men reported that receiving praise served as their motivation for focusing on their partner's orgasm. For many men, sexual performance worked as an act of compensatory masculinity, making up for other areas of their lives where they believed themselves to fall short. Men highly valued praise that placed them above other men in terms of their sexual performance.

Many of the men in this inquiry espoused a belief in a highly sexual identity, and couched their masculinity in terms of it. For them, those two social identities were highly correlated, and they performed them

© The Author(s) 2020
A. M. Walker, *Chasing Masculinity*,
https://doi.org/10.1007/978-3-030-49818-4_8

at a high level. Being in primary partnerships with women who had long ago lost interest in prolonged sexual activity with them proved a difficult reality to navigate and integrate into their identity as very masculine men. Outside partnerships functioned as an outlet to perform that identity and reaffirm themselves as "men."

Compensatory Masculinity

Compensatory masculinity functions as a term to describe those behaviors and practices men engage in to demonstrate their masculinity when they perceive it to be under threat. Typically, men enact these behaviors in response to experiences where they feel unable to perform hegemonic masculinity, and thus perceive their own masculinity to be threatened (Connell, 1987; Connell & Messerschmidt, 2005; Schrock & Schwalbe, 2009; Walker, 2014c). Thus, when facing situations where men feel unable to fully benefit from the "patriarchal dividend" (Connell, 2009), they may choose to "compensate" for their own perceived lack through performance of exaggerated and flashy presentations of manhood (Babl, 1979). Despite the view of men as the most powerful members of society, many perceive themselves as wholly powerless at home or at work, or both (Ezzell, 2012). In short, the patriarchy oppresses everyone; it simply looks differently depending upon your social statuses (e.g. gender, race, class) (hooks, 2004).

Men reported intense pressure to perform sexually, or risk stigma, or even a loss of access to their outside partner. Like masculinity itself, men had to consistently demonstrate sexual prowess. Above all, men appreciated women's claims that they were the "best they ever had." Men who experience feelings of insecurity about their masculinity are "more likely to engage in compensatory behaviors to affirm their masculinity status" (Joseph & Black, 2012; Shumka, Strega, & Hallgrimsdottir, 2017). These men perceived their primary partners as disinterested in them as sexual partners and as people, which served to create insecurity about their status as masculine. Given that a third of the men in this study already believed themselves to lack adequate sexual experience, insecurity loomed for them. Ultimately, like the women in my last book, these men opted to exercise the Infidelity Workaround: outsourcing their unmet needs to an interested third party to avoid the pain, stigma, and expense of a divorce. These men outsourced the emotional aspect of their primary partnerships, much like the seven women in my last book. However, they did so within sexual outside partnerships. For these men, the sexual aspect of their outside partnerships also boosted their sense of themselves as masculine, which in turn increased their sense of self-esteem.

Women's Orgasms as Marker of Masculinity

The scripts around men's sexual behavior demand men's sexual prowess; women's orgasms serve as evidence of men's sexual skill. Women's orgasms function as so central to men's self-perception of their masculinity that women regularly fake orgasms—or feel pressure to do so (Fahs, 2014; Jackson & Scott, 2007; Lafrance, Stelzl, & Bullock, 2017; Rogers, 2005). Men rarely contemplate the probability that their partners faked orgasm, or report an inability to discern between women's orgasm faking and authentic orgasm (Chadwick & Anders, 2017; Cormier & O'Sullivan, 2018; Fahs, 2014; Knox, Zusman, & McNeely, 2008; Leonhardt, Willoughby, Busby, Yorgason, & Holmes, 2018; Roberts et al., 1995), yet research shows women consistently orgasm less often than men (Richters, Visser, Rissel, & Smith, 2006).

Our regard of the importance of women's orgasms shifts over time and place. At present, public discourse promotes women's orgasm as a symbol of both her satisfaction and sexual liberation (Opperman, Brau, Clarke, & Rogers, 2013). However, research shows that both men and women perceive a women's lack of orgasm as troubling mainly due to its impact on the male partner's ego (Salisbury & Fisher, 2014). Further, Salisbury and Fisher found in 2014 that "male and female participants also agreed that men have the physical responsibility to stimulate their female partner to orgasm, while women have the psychological responsibility of being mentally prepared to experience the orgasm" (Salisbury & Fisher, 2014, p. 616). Thus, these men's belief that their responsibilities include the provision of orgasm reflect research. Previous research shows men report women's orgasm as a top sexually satisfying experience

(Braun, Gavey, McPhillips, & McPhillips, 2003). Specifically, men describe experiencing their female partner's orgasm as achievement, an event inspiring self-confidence. Men repeatedly echoed that sentiment throughout our conversations. Sara B. Childers and Sari M. van Anders found in 2017 that "men felt more masculine and reported higher sexual esteem when they imagined that a woman orgasmed during sexual encounters with them, and that this effect was exacerbated for men with high masculine gender role stress" (Chadwick & Anders, 2017). Thus, the researchers concluded that women's orgasms do in fact function as a "masculinity achievement" for men.

Unsurprisingly, this cultural positioning of women's orgasms directly impacts women's experience of them. Women demonstrate awareness of the impact of their orgasm on men. Specifically, women report that concern for their male partner's self-perception as a good lover serves at least part of their desire to orgasm (Fahs, 2014; Lavie & Willig, 2008; Nicolson & Burr, 2003; Salisbury & Fisher, 2014). Thus, we load female orgasm with multiple meanings and purposes, so much so that women's pleasure can be lost entirely. This positioning risks her orgasm becoming pressure-laden rather than wholly pleasurable. Research also shows that women report saving their male partner's ego serves as at least one motivation for faking orgasms (Roberts et al., 1995). The demands of masculinity create dynamics where honest dialogue about sexual needs and pleasure crowd and threaten men's sense of themselves as virile. Men often experience feedback on their performance both as criticism and a suggestion that their masculinity is not up to par. This makes conversations which might actually guide a man to success in orgasm inducement difficult. The mandate of masculinity proves counterproductive and the ability to believe (or pretend to) that she orgasmed becomes more important than her actual experience of pleasure.

"Her Orgasm Evidences My Skill"

The experience of achievement intertwined with discussions of their sexual performance and their partner's orgasm. Failure to evoke orgasm stood as a man's inability to elicit. A woman's experience of orgasm occurred as confirmation of his expertise and competence. Kurt (33, married) elaborated:

> I feel an internal compulsion to GIVE great sex. Obviously, I enjoy sex very much. But my goal in sex is the other person. If I get off, that's great. But if I get off before they do, then it wasn't good sex. I didn't do my job. Even though I finished, I still feel like it wasn't a good experience because they didn't. I'm more of a giver than a taker, you could say.

Notice how his pleasure remains absent from consideration. Sex functions as wholly goal-oriented. If he neglects to evoke her orgasm, then he failed. He justifies this for himself under the guise of being a "giver." However, his behavior aligns with the current mandates for masculinity and sexual skill. The language of being a "giver" permeated the narratives. Kurt (33, married) went on to explain:

> When I'm with a woman, trying my hardest to hold off for just a few more minutes until she collapses into a sweaty heap, it's not because I'm trying to emulate a porn movie, or because that article I read said that I should. It's just natural. It's just what I do.

Here, Kurt reifies the script and his socialization as "natural" and just how he is and "what he does." Yet admits he's exposed to this script detailing the expectations of him as a lover. This language came up repeatedly. Clearly, men internalized the current framing of men's masculinity as demonstrated by sexual performance.

He couched his sexual performance as effort and labor. Many men framed the delivery of female pleasure as their "job." By contrast, in my interviews with women, none of them spoke of sex or evoking orgasm as "work" or their "job." In that study, no woman spoke of feeling responsibility to evoke partner orgasm (Walker, 2018). Yet this idea ran rampant in men's narratives. Todd (36, married) said:

> I'm not a competitive person with others, but I'm very competitive with myself. I do not like to fail, and I get great pleasure from succeeding at my personal goals. Give multiple orgasms to her until she begs me to cum is one of those goals.

Again, we see this framing of evoking orgasm as achievement or accomplishment, and the lack of a partner's orgasm couched as failure. Interestingly, so entrenched was this pressure to perform, the men failed to see it as unusual. Sloan (36, married) said:

> When you spend a lot of time thinking about and/or pursuing sex, you want to think you're good at it. If we aren't, then think of all the wasted time and energy we spend. If I love baking, but if everyone says my cookies are horrible, that's really going to hurt my self-esteem and self-identity after a while.

Here, he equates sex to hobbies rather than a job, but still couches her orgasm in terms of his achievement. And he makes clear that external validation of his efforts matters most. Whether he enjoys the cookies or not, if others openly dislike them, then they must be bad cookies and he can no longer enjoy them. His opinion or experience of them holds no weight. If the cookie tastes good to him, but others say the cookies taste bad, his taste must be wrong, and he now fails to enjoy that cookie. Thus, the opinion of others and their experience of his labor matters far more than his own experience.

Overall, their partner's pleasure served as accomplishment and validation, which they experienced as powerful. Tucker (60, married) said, "For me, I truly enjoy the feeling of my partner's orgasm, especially during cunnilingus. I just feel great to know that I am able to help produce that intensity with my partner." Men spoke of enjoying their partner's orgasm because of what it said about *them* (e.g. "I'm able to help," "I can produce an orgasm in a partner"), not because of any happiness she herself enjoyed. The difference is nuanced, but important.

Some men simply saw their belief of their responsibility to induce female orgasms as an extension of their personality. Gabriel (40, married) added, "I feel pressure to be good at everything. People who accept not being good at anything… that's not an acceptable attitude to me." Under this conception of sexual performance as achievement, their partner's orgasm felt exciting, but it also exists as yet another arena in which to perform, to excel, to achieve. Sean (56, married) said, "[Their orgasm] fulfills that innate desire to please someone and see that pleasure on their face, in their voice, and throughout their body. As a 'giver,' knowing that I can please someone and help them achieve their desires is quite exhilarating." Framing their need to accomplish their partner's orgasm as a personality trait (e.g., "I'm a giver") helped them make sense of their feelings. It also obscured the influence of socialization and social expectations. Couching my own behavior in terms of "this is just my personality" allows me to avoid contextualizing my perceptions and experiences. Instead, I can rely on simplified understandings, and imagine myself as "special" or "unique" rather than the product of my social world. This sense of "this is simply who I am" ran strong. Travis (43, married) explained:

> I think you'd find I'm a "giver." One of my AM [*Ashley Madison*] friends called it a "Superman complex," but I excel, and am happiest when I can provide something for someone else: fulfill their needs, if you like. And I crave the appreciation (sexual and otherwise) that I get in return. To be honest—and what's the point of being here if I'm not honest, right?— I'm a little bit in that mode with you right now. I enjoy the fact that I'm helping you in your study (or, at least, I *think* I'm helping). I feel good about that. Is that too much of an admission?;)

Thus, men internalized the responsibility of competence and manifested that in non-sexual spaces as well. Failing to live up to their responsibility to elicit orgasms incited anxiety and feelings of low self-esteem. For these men, inducing orgasms felt like winning, achieving, accomplishing. This echoes previous research demonstrating that women's orgasm often functions as achievement for men (Chadwick & Anders, 2017; Leonhardt et al., 2018). In fact, research conducted in 2003 found that for some women their desire to experience orgasm existed solely for the sake of their male partners (Nicolson & Burr, 2003). Recent research found that women actually reported higher motivation to ensure that their partner experienced orgasm than men (Barnett, Moore, Woolford, & Riggs, 2018). In a 2019 study of married people in Iran, some men reported that after evoking orgasm in their wives they felt strong, powerful, and masculine (Samadi, Maasoumi, Salehi, Ramezani, & Kohan, 2019).

Interestingly enough, most of the participants invited me to weigh in on my own experience of evoking orgasm as achievement. They often said something along the lines of: "You get it. When you make a guy orgasm, you feel like the most powerful person in the world, right?" Each expressed surprise when I responded that my own experiences lacked any notion of accomplishment or pride when my partner experienced orgasm. Their shock proved so great that we typically exchanged several emails on the topic. I explained, "Given my sexual experiences with men are that my partner routinely orgasms without difficulty, I experience that event as 'typical' or 'unremarkable.' Thus, it doesn't feel like an achievement for me. If it were a less routine event, I might feel differently." Even with that clarification, participants remained unsatisfied with the disparity in our experiences and feelings. Many returned to the point again and again, certain that I simply failed to understand or failed to properly identify or admit my own feelings. Most of the men who pursued this line of inquiry with me seemed extremely disappointed that women don't regard partner orgasm in this way, don't see the production of orgasms as labor, and don't take responsibility for their partner's orgasms. (These men assumed that I spoke for all women, and that my feelings represent all or most women's feelings, even though I stated repeatedly that I could only speak for myself.) So entrenched was this idea of orgasms as an accomplishment, they couldn't imagine a woman wouldn't also feel that way. (Note: In the hundreds of interviews conducted between myself and female participants regarding sexual experiences and perceptions, this idea of men's orgasm as their achievement failed to arise. Women failed to report this concept as a main consideration. This certainly doesn't prove that women don't feel this way or think this way. I don't pretend to know how the bulk of women feel on this topic. I tried to make clear to the participants in this study that I wasn't speaking for anyone but myself.)

It's worth noting here that in my previous book, the bulk of the women (the group who outsourced sexual pleasure to an interested third party) reported their motivation as their own sexual pleasure (Walker, 2018). While they may also value their partner's sexual pleasure as part of the experience, their partner's pleasure failed to eclipse their own (Walker,

2018). Further, many of them explicitly made statements indicating they cared far more about their own pleasure than that of their partners'. For example, Sofia (39, married), who said of her orgasms, "I *take* them like a greedy bitch. And I make no apologies," and Avery (45, married), who said:

> Oh, you wore yourself out giving *me* an orgasm and now you're too tired for yours? Well, too damn bad. Push away from the bacon and run a mile every day, so you'll be better prepared for next time. Improve your stamina. Your orgasm isn't my problem.

This stands in direct contrast to these men's accounts, which clearly position their partner's orgasm as more important and more pleasurable than their own. Framing this as a difference between men and women (i.e., "men are inherently this way and women are not") would be a mistake. This is likely due to a combination of factors. Specifically, the men of this study function under the framework of the expectations of masculinity, which dictate that they prove their prowess via production of female orgasm, and the women referenced existed in sexless and orgasmless primary partnerships, which shaped their approach to and perception of the sexual encounters with their outside partners. Given that, for them, their outside partners functioned as outsourced labor, the women failed to invest in their sexual pleasure in the ways they might within a long-term primary partnership.

These men framed the production of female orgasm as achievement, and as a special ability they possessed, honed, and wielded. To them, agreeing to have sex with a woman included the responsibility to inspire orgasm. They took their assigned tasks seriously. Malcolm (65, married) elaborated:

> I get great pleasure giving a lady a sexual orgasm. I just read that only about 29% of women have an orgasm during sex. I feel that's terrible. I go out of my way to make sure that the lady has multiple orgasms.

Again, men's research on women's sexuality influenced their behavior. Men truly felt obligated to produce orgasm within their outside partners, a feat they failed to accomplish with primary partners. The fact that outside partners arrived willing and enthusiastic, met with them at great personal risk, and continued seeing them out of desire rather than an obligation (i.e., they lacked an obligation to remain with the men like their primary partners) may have increased men's sense of responsibility as well.

The men's outlook and goals within these outside partnerships contrast with the existing research on men's behavior and aims within hookups on college campuses, which found that men's reluctance and refusal to perform oral sex accounts for much of the orgasm gap within hookup contexts (Armstrong, England, & Fogarty, 2012). However, these findings are consistent with data showing men in marriages and long-term pairings see their partner's orgasm as important to their own experience and pleasure, as a measure of their masculinity, and as their responsibility (Braun et al., 2003; Fahs, 2014; Jackson & Scott, 2007; Lafrance et al., 2017; Rogers, 2005). Given that men in this sample repeatedly spoke of their intent and desire to form ongoing, long-term outside partnerships, their framing, and perception of their responsibility to provide pleasure to their partner makes sense. Additionally, given that in my previous work with women on *Ashley Madison*, women stated that they quickly discarded those men who failed to provoke their orgasm (Walker, 2018), the men in this study may have adopted this outlook during their participation in outside partners even if they failed to hold the belief prior to participation. Further, a 2018 study found that women who considered sexual duration (i.e., time between penetration and partner ejaculation) important were more likely to report breakups; specifically, these women reported their partner's stamina as crucial to their ability to orgasm as well as their quality of orgasm (Burri, Buchmeier, & Porst, 2018). If men's dating and relationship history includes women who broke off the relationship due to their inability to elicit orgasm—due to lack of stamina or another cause— they may internalize the idea that their responsibilities include provision of orgasm. Further, as previously discussed, the U.S. cultural mandates around masculinity demand heterosexual sexual prowess, demonstrated through their partner's orgasm.

These men worked at discovering better ways to make their partners orgasm. Many men spoke of statistics and facts gleaned through research into women's bodies and orgasms. Malcolm (65, married) added:

> Giving sexual pleasure is my hobby. I have often referred to myself as "Doctor." In my mind, a female has a problem. She wants to have sexual pleasure, and her husband, boyfriend or whomever, cannot or will not help her. So, I will help her as best I can. I think of myself as a male whore (without pay). Sometimes I even think it is my job, and I want to do a good job.

Here he positions himself as the man with the solution. He sees his partner's lack of orgasm as a problem he is uniquely suited to solve—and one that he solves better than other men. He expresses concern for the orgasm gap, and awareness of his partner's needs. By doing so, he shows himself as sexually skilled. When men included their outside partner's pleasure in their discussions of these experiences, they still framed that as proof of their skills. Malcolm added, "I enjoy the juices that I can drink from a woman." Notice on the surface he's sharing something he enjoys, but within that is the suggestion that he is skilled enough to induce orgasms and pleasure (i.e., "juices").

For many men, this sense of responsibility and their corresponding ability to meet their duties felt sacred. They experienced every partner's orgasm as proof of their worth, and their masculinity. Riley (39, married) explained of an outside partner:

> [My outside partner] is 45 and had never before enjoyed sex, had poor sexual partners, had never allowed herself to explore her own sexuality, even in her imagination. She has let me show her things about intimacy and sex, reveal things to her about herself that I could feel were inside her. I have been able to give her that safe place to explore anything and celebrate what we find. That is the most fulfilling feeling in my life: to do that for someone.

When we look more closely at this statement, something interesting reveals itself. Again, we see the concern for the orgasm gap and his partner's needs, and the man's self-presentation as problem-solver.

He "showed" her things, "revealed things to her about herself." Men spoke in these terms often in our discussions, never once hearing themselves and noticing the obvious savior narrative. He positions his special skills and his expertise in sexual matters as completely responsible for her sexual awakening. The undergirding assumption here is that if he had never come along, never chosen her as his sexual partner, she would never have discovered this. This positions her sexual experience with him as priceless, precious, and her as lucky to have been chosen by him. His phrase "things about herself that I could feel were inside her" proves telling. Many of the men I spoke to genuinely believed themselves to hold special sexual secrets, the keys to women's sexual liberation, and an ability to know a woman better than she knew herself, to see untapped sexual possibilities within her. They often suggested an ability to know of deeply seated sexual preferences of hers, of which she was unaware. Further, they frequently positioned their partners as never having had good or satisfying sex prior to sex with them. When pressed as to whether she had stated this, most men admitted they assumed this without any indication from their partner. While it may be easy to see these men negatively in light of the narratives they present, we must remember that they make these statements and frame their experiences in these ways under the weight of the burden of U.S. modern masculinity's demands of men. Previous research into women's experiences echo these men's perceptions as well (Montemurro, 2014; Waskul, Vannini, & Wiesen, 2007). In a world that demands sexual prowess of men to be considered masculine, when men find themselves in primary partnerships lacking adequate praise of their sexual skill—and encounters suggest a lack of prowess—men *needed* outside partners to provide evidence of their manliness. If outside partners failed to verbalize high praise, men sometimes assumed it for themselves. Again, these are acts of compensatory masculinity. Men framed encounters through the lens of their own sexual skill in an effort to reassure themselves that they're adequately masculine. While it's easy to write the concerns of these men off as silly or trivial, it's important to remember the social pressure in the United States for men to be manly and that sexual prowess functions as evidence of such.

Her Pleasure Is My Pleasure

Given the current U.S. cultural framing of women's orgasms as indicative of men's sexual skills, it's perhaps predictable that men reported deriving their pleasure from that of their partners. Men's own pleasure in their own orgasm was wholly absent from these narratives. Brock (32, married) said:

> I do feel pressure to be a stud. It may be my need to please people and to be loved that drives me. I genuinely feel happy bringing a woman to orgasm. Not sure why but I feel better making someone else climax than I do myself. Is that weird? I always want to go down on a girl and make sure that she comes more than once before I let her do anything to me. I, personally, want to be good at it so that my partner experiences pleasure with me. This is a huge turn-on for me. I love to bring my partner to orgasm.

As previously discussed, the idea of deriving your sexual pleasure from your partner's is fairly common in U.S. public discourse. On the surface, it seems positive and female-centered. However, in practice it can result in pressure on women to fake orgasms in an effort to soothe male partner's egos, and in men framing sex as achievement rather than an act of pleasure. We celebrate and reward men who espouse this view of pleasure, acting as though this ensures women's pleasure and indicates that men better value their female sexual partners as people. (Note: in some situations, it may well ensure that.)

While on the surface this narrative of "my pleasure comes from their pleasure" may seem positive for women's sexuality, men aren't the only recipients of that message. Young women often internalize the idea that only your partner's orgasm counts, regarding concern for their own pleasure as selfish (Armstrong et al., 2012). Many young women report having never experienced orgasm even while alone, but they expressed no concern about this (Fahs, 2014). So committed to the idea that their partner's pleasure is *their* pleasure, they see a lifetime of inorgasmic sex as acceptable. Meanwhile, existing research shows that many men experience their own orgasms as less pleasurable than the knowledge that their masculinity remains intact as evidenced by their partner's orgasm—even when that evidence is often faked. So, while the temptation may be to brush off these men's narratives, they echo the feelings of many men in the U.S. context.

Given U.S. cultural messages equating the provocation of women's orgasm with masculinity, men's internalization of their partner's pleasure as pleasure for themselves makes sense (Lewington, Sebar, & Lee, 2018; Porter, Douglas, & Collumbien, 2016). Men I spoke with genuinely believed that their focus on their partner's pleasure was simply "how I am," and rejected any notions that these ideas may have come from an external source of socialization. Rudy (42, married) explained:

> My earliest sexual intercourse experiences were not very satisfying, as I was quick to orgasm, and my partner seemed disappointed that it was over already. Oral sex experiences always lasted longer, so it was frustrating that intercourse sex for me did not take long. Once I started to manually or orally stimulate my partner to an orgasm, I learned that it was a bigger turn-on for me to witness her orgasm knowing I had a part in it, and the more she reacted (squirmed, thrashed, cried out, etc.) the more turned on I became, and then the more satisfied I was when we had intercourse.

Rudy describes developing this framing of his partner's pleasure as his own as both simple fact, and something he "learned," implying that he gained this awareness through experience and age. For him, this is "simply how things are," emblematic of most social constructs. Byron (57, married) added, "It is rewarding to provide the pleasure to a partner that they otherwise would not receive. Unfortunately, there are a lot of lonely people out there and if I can alleviate some of that loneliness, it gives me satisfaction." Again, we see the framing of responsibility and charity. This permits men to see themselves as both masculine and a good guy. The experience of providing her pleasure did wonders for their esteem. Salvador (53, married) said:

> It means a lot to me to be able to satisfy a woman and that's how I get my satisfaction: the knowing, feeling her quiver, so I can get more experience. As you know better than I, women are emotional and men are visual/physical. So, when I can really have a woman sexually satisfied,

I get great pleasure afterwards. It really makes me feel good to have her in my arms afterwards just holding her as she falls asleep!!!!

These narratives hinge on strong tethering to gender norms (e.g., "women are emotional; men are visual"), which reify the expectations of masculinity. For many men in this inquiry, their deliverance of orgasms is akin to public service or charity work. After all, they're doing the work other men failed to do. Once again, we must consider their statements through the lens of the demands of masculinity. (Note: I in no way mean to suggest that the gaining of sexual technique and awareness that many women need more than penetrative vaginal intercourse to orgasm is negative.)

Doing It for the Praise

Their partner's response to their performance played an important role in how men viewed themselves. The need to please and to be praised for that proved salient. Men reported that praise for their aptitude to bring their partner to orgasm functioned as a strong motivator. Byron (57, married) added:

I would like to think that those extra partners enjoy our experiences together as well. Based on their reactions and comments, they certainly seem to. One woman told me that my wife was a fool for not wanting me more after we made love four times within about 14 hours. I have had several tell me that my cock was larger than average. One actually called it a monster.

The men soaked up the praise of their skills and their bodies. Compliments about their penis specifically existed as treasured feedback. Several men specifically shared numerous accounts of compliments regarding their penis size, appearance, and function. For men who view their sexual performance as a responsibility and orgasms as their performance review, compliments and praise proved valuable. Rudy (42, married) said:

> I want to be great at sex because I learned that I enjoy getting my partner to orgasm, and I also enjoyed some of the praise that I received from partners. Not all of them, though I would say I'm pretty good since no one ever laughed me out of bed. Those that did compliment me, either in-person or online, were also partners that I was able to bring to a full orgasm.

The connection for men was clear and obvious: when they induced orgasms, women spoke highly of them, and wanted to see them again. Men badly needed that praise.

For men whose primary partners failed to experience orgasm with them, outside partnerships offered a shot at redemption. Gabriel (40, married) said, "Big thing for me was orgasms for my outside partner. It bothers me that [my wife] can't orgasm with me." For men in this situation, the ability to bring another woman to orgasm helped negate the hurt and feelings of doubt inspired by their wife's inability to orgasm, yet their failure at home still weighed on them. Everett (42, married) added, "My problems stem from being unable to please my wife and it hurts me because I'm unable to give her an orgasm, something that's so easy for me [with other women]." For these men, performing with outside partners helped boost flagging self-esteem. However, there remained the need to make *every* partner orgasm—or at least both their wife and their outside partner. Sex with outside partners served as a space where their masculinity could be validated through their partner's orgasms. The more praise their partners heaped upon them, the greater their sense of themselves as capable lovers and proficient men. However, shame at their perceived failure in their marital beds lingered.

Best They Ever Had

Men prided themselves on besting the "average man's" performance, which they believed to be lackluster. Anderson (50, married) described this:

> I have been told by just about every woman I have slept with that I am
> the most amazing lover they have ever had. (They say it, not me.) There
> are so many guys out there [who] are in it for a quick 3-pump-chump-
> fuck and it gives guys a bad name. I always want to be the best fuck any
> woman has ever had. So, I guess the pressure comes from me internally.
> I am really good at sex (so I have been told many times). I have a larger
> penis than the average man (so I have been told). And I have amazing
> staying power and control.

Anderson took great pride in his rave reviews. He pressured himself to
always deliver a top-notch performance. While he believed he possessed
the attributes he perceived as necessary to provide good sex (i.e., skill,
penis size, stamina), he still valued his partners' declarations of "best they
ever had."

Given that the circumstances of forming and keeping outside partnerships included fierce competition with other men on *Ashley Madison*—a
situation that both the men in this study and the women in the former
study perceive as placing the power and control squarely in women's
laps—men felt compelled to be "the best" in bed (Walker, 2018).
Men employed sexual prowess as a strategy to enable them to maintain ongoing outside partnerships. However, they also worked for the
praise of these women. Anderson explained, "Maybe just for the charge
I get when we are done and she says something like 'What the hell
was that? Oh my God, what did you just do to me?'" Thus, showing
acumen in sexual performance separated them from the pack. Many men
experienced this as an accomplishment.

For men who fail to induce orgasm in their wives, gaining the praise of
an outside partner proved important. If a woman touted them as "best I
ever had," all the better. Brock (32, married) explained, "I love being the
one who can make them climax, who is the best kisser, the most attentive
lover." Making their partner orgasm functioned as validation for these
men. Besting all other men increased the ego boost, but also served as an
assurance that the outside partner will continue to see him, continue to
grant him the opportunity to perform his masculinity. Again, we see this
narrative of men holding special sexual knowledge and skill, and doling
it out benevolently.

However, every encounter offered both the opportunity for possible victory and failure. Riley (39, married) explained:

> You think you're supposed to look like a movie star, and fuck like a porn star. Like you're supposed to have this huge dick and be able to pound away on some poor girl for 20-40 minutes, and then cum on command. If I've been blessed enough to get my chance to show a woman why she wants to be with me, I will make an impression.

In these narratives about the competitive nature of men's sexual performance in outside partnerships, we can see clearly much of this really has nothing to do with the women themselves. Riley continues:

> In some cases, I know I go too far, do too much. Even if I can feel that my partner wants a nice simple orgasm and cuddle until falling asleep, I'll feel compelled to give her multiple orgasms, and [cause her to] lose the power of speech and possibly breathing.

He admits that he's aware of her wishes, but he cannot help himself. He must outdo any other potential lovers. He must deliver the most earth-shattering performance he can muster—even if that's counter to what she actually wants at that moment. This echoes Rachel O'Neill's 2018 work which found that among men who invest in the outlook that men's skills at seduction function as an art form, women's "last minute resistance" (LMR) exists as only token resistance, a part of the game, if you will (O'Neill, 2018). Media messages often present the idea that sex functions as a game of pursuit where men should prevail and show acumen (Wood, 2009). Under this framework, "men must figure out how to work around any barriers a woman puts in place to prevent sex" or whatever sexual act he intends (Keith, 2017, p. 226). Lest we think that men are simply clueless about their behavior, Riley clarifies:

> I'm smart enough to understand that when I do that, it's not even about her. It's about me and my issues and insecurities, and that's not fair. But in the grand scheme, I guess it's good that the end result for my partner is amazing sex, and a lot of it.

So, these men often understood what they were really doing, but continued to justify their own behavior. At the end of the day, being told they were "the best I ever had" proved too seductive to *not* pursue. This speaks to the depth of men's need for praise. Matteo (44, married) said:

> I only hear two things about my performance, and one of them is how deficient the [outside partner]'s sex is elsewhere. And that in itself is an unaccounted secret gift to me. Truly, the secret to great sex is the confident masculinity of the man and his ability to interpret the sexual needs/language of the woman.

Matteo believed that the ability to deliver great sex required masculinity, as well as special skills unavailable to all men. Again, we see the positioning of the man as a sexual savant, a holder of special sexual knowledge and skills, which he doles out benevolently.

One man actually contacted me after his interview had officially ended to tell me a rather lengthy story about a recent encounter. He took great pains to describe meeting a woman whom he claimed to find not remotely attractive. He then went on to talk at length about his decision to go ahead and have sex with her—for hours, of course—out of charity. He assumed she was so unattractive and hard-up that she likely never got sex. In his mind, he did her a kindness by delivering "great sex" for a few hours, and then never contacting her again. He spoke with pride and obvious joy regarding his decision-making, sexual performance, and charitable nature. In his mind, he gave her the gift of his amazing prowess and the best sex of her life. Incidentally, he got angry with me due to my lack of enthusiastic response to his tale and quickly resorted to name-calling. He then sent a message saying he deeply regretted participating in the study, and requested I never speak to him again. I obliged, and removed his interview data from this study as well. His upset with me stemmed from my failure to validate his altruism and to commend him for providing this woman with the "best sex she'd ever had." For this participant, the study had effectively ended, yet he felt it important to reach out with additional data regarding both his prowess and his altruism with regard to providing quality sexual experiences. In his mind, his provision of "best sex ever" to a woman he truly perceived as homely further cemented his status as both masculine and a good guy. My silence regarding his afternoon of what he saw as charity work challenged this perception of himself.

This narrative of responsibility to provide orgasms, and how that shapes men's self-perception as well as their interactions with women proved salient. The men in this study felt it important to communicate to the researcher their high level of sexual skill, as evidenced by partner orgasm and praise. This echoes 2015 research by a team led by Sapna Cheryan which found that men react to perceived threats to their masculinity by exaggerating their masculinity. Through claiming they are the "best [their outside partners] ever had," the men in this study accomplish the same thing. That praise serves as important after the failure to provoke orgasm for their primary partners, experiences which function as a threat. Michael Flood's 2007 study found that for men, sexual activity functions as a pathway to masculine status, and it is other men—"always imagined and sometimes real"—who serve as the audience for this performance (Flood, 2007). And 2012 research by a team led by William Elder showed that men perceived themselves as in competition with other men for the sexual attention of women (Elder, Brooks, & Morrow, 2012). (Because men truly believed they so outnumbered women on *Ashley Madison,* these men felt that acutely. However, in reality the ratio of men to women on the site is comparable.) For the men in this sample, hearing outside partners proclaim them as "the best I've ever had" generated an imaginary audience of other men, against whom they imagine themselves competing.

Self-Perception of High Sex Drive

Of the 46 men who participated in this study, roughly 33% (15 men) of them spoke specifically of having a high sex drive. These men reported a sense of themselves as particularly interested in sexual activity. Mike (53, married) noted, "I am super sexual!!!" Often they explained that their perception stood in comparison to other men. Brock (32, married) "I just have an unusually high sex drive (at least compared with some of my friends)." It's important to remember that these men strongly adhered to gender expectations, which position men as much more interested in sex than women. So, this subgroup of men believed themselves to be beyond even the elevated interest of men in general.

This sense of having a "high sex drive" served as an identity of sorts. Holden (41, married) described himself this way: "Sensuality and lust pours from me. I try to find outlets for it that are more inane. I write erotica (I'm really good, btw). I fantasize, and spend more time thinking about sex than almost anything else." This identity manifested itself in behaviors confirming their high drive. Anderson (50, married) added, "I love sex, lots of it! I masturbate daily, sometimes twice, because I just love the feeling of an orgasm. I have sex usually once a day, also sometimes twice including the whacking. :)" For these men, their sense of themselves as highly sexual dominated their identity.

For men whose primary partners lost interest in sensuality and extended sexual sessions over time, this "high sex drive" functioned as a challenge. Jake (48, married) said, "She has gone through the 'change' and sex doesn't interest her as much, and my sex drive is still rather high." When their spouse lost interest, these men reported difficulty in going without. Rudy (42, married) added:

> [My] high sex drive initially had me doing a lot of fantasizing about past relationships/sexual encounters and masturbating to those fantasies. That satisfied me for a time but [my need] grew to the point that I decided to seek an outside partner relationship.

The men in this subgroup partly faulted their "high sex drive" with the decision to seek out an outside partner, despite the fact that by their own admission they more highly valued the relational management and praise gained than the sexual pleasure.

These men believed no one could keep up with them. Holden (41, married) added, "I knew that I'd be the one who would be wanting it more, and that I'd be a better lover than my wife. I knew that she would have no complaints." Within these narratives, we see the same positioning of themselves as having sexual gifts they charitably bestow on their partners. Holden clearly believes that his partners have no room for complaints because he is such a talented lover. He also assumes he will always be the party who is disappointed in the sexual relationship.

For one man, his highly sexual identity justified his participation in infidelity, which served as a relationship strategy throughout his life. Malcolm (65, married) elaborated:

> I was having external relationships while she was pregnant and after we married. I enjoyed sex immensely. I never had what I considered an affair. My definition of an affair is something that continues for a length of time, love is potentially involved, and is rather in competition with your marriage. I love my wife, but I have sex with other women. It is my "hobby." I don't drink, play golf, go out with the boys, or anything else. I enjoy having sex.

Malcolm believed that his current behavior simply expressed who he really is. As a result of this mindset and practices, he reported a rather high partner count. He said, "Over the past 8 months, I have enjoyed about 170 girls (Of course, some many times)." For a time, his quest bordered on the obsessive. He added, "In the beginning, I was looking for quantity. I found myself giving oral to 4, 5, 6, and as many as 7 girls in a day." But eventually, he settled into a more sustainable pace. "I then started to only see for the third or more times, girls that I felt really were enjoying themselves, and I was enjoying them." It's worth mentioning that this participant reported an inability to perform penetrative sexual intercourse. He explained, "I am at the point in my life that I suffer from ED [erectile dysfunction] for the last 15 years or so." Thus, his encounters included providing pleasure for his partner, but no release for him. When pressed about this, he explained that for him pleasure came from giving his partner pleasure. So, he internalized the current narrative around sexual pleasure. Malcolm may be engaging in compensatory masculinity as he may experience his erectile dysfunction as emasculating (Keith, 2017).

Conclusion

Men reported a sense of responsibility for providing women's orgasms, in part because of their belief in their own exceptionality with regard to their sexual prowess. Simultaneously, women's orgasms served as an achievement for which they felt tremendous pride. Men perceived themselves as special due to their ability to induce orgasms for their partners. They reported experiencing their partner's pleasure as their own pleasure. Yet their own orgasms remained mostly absent in these discussions, as though they lack importance.

Men's narratives about participation in outside partnerships make clear their concerns regarding performing well sexually, avoiding the stigma attached to poor performance, gaining praise, and being desired. Sexual encounters with outside partners offered respite from the hurtful sexual encounters with wives who approached sex as a chore—or marriages that were entirely sexless—and offered outlets for unmet sexual desires, but also applied pressure in men's lives. Men who enjoyed success in these spaces enjoyed the praise of outside partners, especially praise labeling them as "best I ever had." Scripts surrounding masculinity are embedded within these narratives, shaping and guiding men's behavior.

A small subset of men in this study framed themselves as highly sexual. Their self-perception hinged on this identity of extremely virile and sexually motivated. Given the tendency of this group to conform to gender expectations, which include the narrative that men are inherently more sexual than women, these men placed themselves above the average man in terms of sexual interest. They perceived this trait as so salient that others could pick up on it as well.

References

Armstrong, E. A., England, P., & Fogarty, A. C. K. (2012). Accounting for women's orgasm and sexual enjoyment in college hookups and relationships. *American Sociological Review, 77*(3), 435–462. https://doi.org/10.1177/000 3122412445802.

Babl, J. D. (1979). Compensatory masculine responding as a function of sex role. *Journal of Consulting and Clinical Psychology, 47,* 252–257.

Barnett, M. D., Moore, J. M., Woolford, B. A., & Riggs, S. A. (2018). Interest in partner orgasm: Sex differences and relationships with attachment strategies. *Personality and Individual Differences, 124*(1), 194–200. https://doi.org/10.1016/j.paid.2017.12.015.

Braun, V., Gavey, N., McPhillips, K., & McPhillips, K. (2003). The 'fair deal'? Unpacking accounts of reciprocity in heterosex. *Sexualities, 6*(2), 237–261. https://doi.org/10.1177/1363460703006002005.

Burri, A., Buchmeier, J., & Porst, H. (2018). The importance of male ejaculation for female sexual satisfaction and function. *Journal of Sexual Medicine, 15*(7), S123. https://doi.org/10.1016/j.jsxm.2018.04.005.

Chadwick, S. B., & Anders, S. M. v. (2017). Do women's orgasms function as a masculinity achievement for men? *The Journal of Sex Research, 54*(9), 1141–1152. https://doi.org/10.1080/00224499.2017.1283484.

Connell, R. W. (1987). *Gender and power*. Sydney: Allen and Urwi.

Connell, R. W. (2009). *Short introductions: Gender*. Malden, MA: Polity.

Connell, R. W., & Messerschmidt, J. W. (2005). Hegemonic masculinity: Rethinking the concept. *Gender and Society, 19*(6), 829–859. https://doi.org/10.1177/0891243205278639.

Cormier, L. A., & O'Sullivan, L. F. (2018). Anti-climactic: Investigating how late adolescents perceive and deal with orgasm difficulty in the context of their intimate relationships. *The Canadian Journal of Human Sexuality, 27*(2), 111–122. https://doi.org/10.3138/cjhs.2018-001.

Elder, W. B., Brooks, G. R., & Morrow, S. (2012). Sexual self-schemas of heterosexual men. *Psychology of Men & Masculinity, 13*(2), 166–179. https://doi.org/10.1037/a0024835.

Ezzell, M. B. (2012). "I'm in control": Compensatory manhood in a therapeutic community. *Gender & Society, 26*(2), 190–215. https://doi.org/10.1177/0891243211434611126.

Fahs, B. (2014). Coming to power: Women's fake orgasms and best orgasm experiences illuminate the failures of (hetero)sex and the pleasures of connection. *Culture, Health & Sexuality, 16*(8), 974–988. https://doi.org/10.1080/13691058.2014.924557.

Flood, M. (2007). Men, sex, and homosociality: How bonds between men shape their sexual relations with women. *Men and Masculinities, 10*(3), 339–359. https://doi.org/10.1177/1097184X06287761.

hooks, b. (2004). *Will to change: Men, masculinity, and love*. New York, NY: Washington Square Press.

Jackson, S., & Scott, S. (2007). Faking like a woman? Towards an interpretive theorization of sexual pleasure. *Body & Society, 13,* 95–116. https://doi.org/10.1177/1357034X07077777.

Joseph, L. J., & Black, P. (2012). Who's the man? Fragile masculinities, consumer masculinities, and the profiles of sex work clients. *Men and Masculinities, 15*(5), 486–506. https://doi.org/10.1177/1097184X12458591.

Keith, T. (2017). *Masculinities in contemporary American culture.* New York: Routledge.

Knox, D., Zusman, M., & McNeely, A. (2008). University student beliefs about sex: Men vs. women. *College Student Journal, 42*(1), 181–185.

Lafrance, M. N., Stelzl, M., & Bullock, K. (2017). "I'm not gonna fake it": University women's accounts of resisting the normative practice of faking orgasm. *Psychology of Women Quarterly, 41*(2), 210–222. https://doi.org/10.1177/0361684316683520.

Lavie, M., & Willig, C. (2008). "I don't feel like melting butter": An interpretative phenomenological analysis of the experience of "inorgasmia." *20*(1), 115–128 https://doi.org/10.1080/08870440412331296044.

Leonhardt, N. D., Willoughby, B. J., Busby, D. M., Yorgason, J. B., & Holmes, E. K. (2018). The significance of the female orgasm: A nationally representative, dyadic study of newlyweds' orgasm experience. *The Journal of Sexual Medicine, 15*(8), 1140–1148. https://doi.org/10.1016/j.jsxm.2018.05.018.

Lewington, L., Sebar, B., & Lee, J. (2018). "Becoming the man you always wanted to be": Exploring the representation of health and masculinity in Men's Health magazine. *Health Promotion Journal of Australia.* https://doi.org/10.1002/hpja.204.

Montemurro, B. (2014). *Deserving desire: Women's stories of sexual evolution.* New Brunswick, NJ: Rutgers University Press.

Nicolson, P., & Burr, J. (2003). What is "normal" about women's (hetero) sexual desire and orgasm? A report of an in-depth interview study. *Social Science and Medicine, 57*(9), 1735–1745. https://doi.org/10.1016/S0277-9536(03)00012-1.

O'Neill, R. (2018). *Seduction: Men, masculinity and mediated intimacy.* Cambridge, UK: Polity.

Opperman, E., Brau, V., Clarke, V., & Rogers, C. (2013). "It feels so good it almost hurts": Young adults' experiences of orgasm and sexual pleasure. *Journal of Sex Research, 51*(5), 503–515. https://doi.org/10.1080/00224499.2012.753982.

Porter, C. N., Douglas, N., & Collumbien, M. (2016). 'Enhance her pleasure - and your grip strength': Men's Health magazine and pseudo-reciprocal pleasure. *Culture Health & Sexuality, 19*(7), 1–14. https://doi.org/10.1080/13691058.2016.1258591.

Richters, J., Visser, R. d, Rissel, C., & Smith, A. (2006). Sexual practices at last heterosexual encounter and occurrence of orgasm in a national survey. *The Journal of Sex Research, 43*(3), 217–226. https://doi.org/10.1080/00224490609552320.

Roberts, C., Kippax, S., Kippax, S., Waldby, C., Waldby, C., & Crawford, J. (1995). Faking it: The story of "ohh!". *Women's Studies International Forum, 18*(5/6), 523–553. https://doi.org/10.1016/0277-5395(95)80090-C.

Rogers, A. (2005). Chaos to control: Men's magazines and the mastering of intimacy. *Men and Masculinities, 8*(2), 175–194. https://doi.org/10.1177/1097184X04265319.

Salisbury, C. M. A., & Fisher, W. A. (2014). "Did you come?" A qualitative exploration of gender differences in beliefs, experiences, and concerns regarding female orgasm occurrence during heterosexual sexual interactions. *The Journal of Sex Research, 51*(6), 616–631. https://doi.org/10.1080/00224499.2013.838934.

Samadi, P., Maasoumi, R., Salehi, M., Ramezani, M. A., & Kohan, S. (2019). Married women's and men's experiences regarding the concept of sexual desire: A qualitative research. *Iranian Journal of Psychiatry and Behavioral Sciences, 13*(1), e66324. https://doi.org/10.5812/ijpbs.66324.

Schrock, D., & Schwalbe, M. (2009). Men, masculinity, and manhood acts. *Annual Review of Sociology, 35,* 277–295. https://doi.org/10.1146/annurev-soc-070308-115933.

Shumka, L., Strega, S., & Hallgrimsdottir, H. K. (2017). "I wanted to feel like a man again": Hegemonic masculinity in relation to the purchase of street-level sex. *Frontiers in Sociology, 2*(15). https://doi.org/10.3389/fsoc.2017.00015.

Walker, A. M. (2014a). "I'm not a lesbian; I'm just a freak": A pilot study of the experiences of women in assumed-monogamous other-sex unions seeking secret same-sex encounters online, their negotiation of sexual desire, and meaning-making of sexual identity. *Sexuality and Culture, 18*(4), 911–935. https://doi.org/10.1007/s12119-014-9226-5.

Walker, A. M. (2014b). 'Our little secret': How publicly heterosexual women make meaning from their 'undercover' same-sex sexual experiences. *Journal of Bisexuality, 14*(2), 194–208. https://doi.org/10.1080/15299716.2014.902347.

Walker, A. M. (2014c). Revenge of the Beta Boys: Opting out as an exercise in masculinity. *McGill Journal of Education, 49*(1), 183–2000.

Walker, A. M. (2018). *The secret life of the cheating wife: Power, pragmatism, and pleasure in women's infidelity.* Lanham, MD: Lexington Books.

Waskul, D. D., Vannini, P., & Wiesen, D. (2007). Women and their clitoris: Personal discovery, significance, and use. *Symbolic Interaction, 30.* https://doi.org/10.1525/si.2007.30.2.151.

Wood, J. T. (2009). *Gendered lives: Communication, gender, and culture.* Boston, MA: Cengage.

9

So, What Does All of This Mean Anyway?: Making Sense of Men's Participation in Infidelity

In the United States, sex sells, but infidelity *really* sells. So long as the individual isn't the one discovering infidelity in their own relationship, the public eats up news of cheating. Americans greedily consume stories of suspected unfaithfulness from celebrity pairings to neighbors to politicians to coworkers. Even the details of total strangers' cheating demand their attention (e.g., friends of friends). Through these stories, Americans reaffirm a shared cultural commitment to monogamy and to being a "good" person, which includes being a person who doesn't cheat. Social scripts portray men as deeply sexually preoccupied and desirous of a variety of sexual partners, and, therefore, prone to cheat. Thus, while Americans gobble up stories of men's extra-relational escapades, they also see the behavior as commonplace and expected. The idea that "men are dogs" runs rampant through public and private discourse. The assumption remains that men cheat simply because they can, and that any man offered an opportunity for sex will act on it. We assume men cheat for the opportunity to have sex with a new partner. The men in this inquiry challenge those assumptions and commonsense understandings.

I'd certainly heard all of the commonsense understandings of men's outside partnerships. As a researcher, I wondered if that really was the

© The Author(s) 2020
A. M. Walker, *Chasing Masculinity*,
https://doi.org/10.1007/978-3-030-49818-4_9

whole story. I sought to learn whether men felt their participation in infidelity merely served as a sexual release with a new partner, or if they had other motives for their behavior. I wasn't sure what I'd find. I wasn't sure men would be willing to speak with a female researcher about their deepest, darkest sexual secrets. To my shock and delight, men proved enthusiastic about sharing their lives with me.

Implications for Clinical Practice

These narratives clearly show that men's perceptions of the dynamics within their primary partnerships influenced their decision to seek out and participate in outside partnerships. However, unlike many of the women in my previous study, these men maintained monogamy in their outside partnerships. They consistently and repeatedly said, "I'm looking for *one* woman devoted to me" with regard to their outside partnerships. Men reported that while sexual, these outside partnerships served to soothe their bruised egos, address unmet emotional needs, provide relational management, and reify their own sense of themselves as masculine. Specifically, men complained that their wives failed to pay them enough attention, give enough praise for their contributions and efforts, demonstrate interest in their days and feelings, and failed to show enthusiasm and passion in their sexual encounters, which the men experienced as emasculating. Men believed that if they were better lovers, their wives would bring passion and eagerness into bed.

Given that in the United States, we assume men's infidelity motives to be sexual, this proves useful. How many other men feel similarly? Keep in mind that when initially asked the reason for their infidelity, men focused on sexual motivations, hiding behind gendered socialization that tells men they are "inherently" sexually preoccupied and desire large partner counts. But as these men talked more, they revealed that their motivations stemmed from their perceptions of disinterest on the part of their primary partners and their hurt that she denied them the time, attention, and praise they craved. We cannot know how accurate men's perceptions of their marriages are without also speaking to their wives—an impossibility as it threatens confidentiality and risks the revelation of the men's outside partnerships. However, as the Thomas Theorem explains, "facts" don't exist apart from our observance and interpretation of them. What is real to us are the ways we define situations for ourselves. In other words, "if men define situations as real, they are real in their consequences" (Thomas & Thomas, 1928). Thus, for the men, what they report is the reality. Perhaps in a therapeutic setting the accuracy of such perceptions could be addressed.

Masculinity played a role in men's participation in outside partnerships. The ways in which they experienced emasculation in response to the events in their home lives proves important and relevant for therapeutic settings. Without speaking to their wives, I can only assume their primary partners likely have no idea that these men perceive these interactions as a blow to their sense of themselves as men. Additionally, the men's perceptions of their wives' boredom and disinterest in them as sexual partners proved important as well. Men experience this as proof of waning or absent masculinity, but existing research shows this may well be a function of shared living quarters over time (Klusmann, 2002). In other words, the current research establishes that for women, familiarity kills libido. For counselors and therapists working with couples on this issue, perhaps some workarounds could be devised to reignite the perceived missing passion and enthusiasm. Further, and perhaps most importantly, men could be made to understand that the decline doesn't reliably signal anything about the men themselves, but may simply speak to the nature of modern life, shared living spaces, and the function of women's libido (Graham et al., 2017; Gunst, Ventus, Kärnä, Salo, & Jern, 2016; Klusmann, 2002, 2006; Morton & Gorzalka, 2014; Sims & Meana, 2010).

Just as men expected their primary partners to help manage their emotional lives through relational management, men appreciated the provision of relational management of their outside partners. This has implications for therapeutic settings as well. Discussions regarding the burden placed on women, and the development of tools for men to better manage their own emotional lives proves necessary for happier, healthier long-term pairings. Unlike the women of previous studies, the overwhelming majority of men expressed emotional attachment to outside partners and approached their pairings with great sentimentality.

This challenges previous work claiming that women tend to participate in "emotional affairs" and tend to "fall in love" with their partners, while men tend to seek out sexual affairs only (Banfield & McCabe, 2001; Glass & Wright, 1985; Spanier & Margolis, 1983). This has implications for clinical practice. Ultimately, these men, like the women in the previous study, sought the Infidelity Workaround: they attempted to outsource their unmet needs to an interested third party while avoiding the pain, stigma, and expense of a divorce. Like the small minority of women in my previous book whose primary partnerships failed to meet their need for emotional support and intimacy, these men also sought to outsource their unmet emotional needs. The outsourcing took place within sexual relationships. However, the most prized benefit of these partnerships remained the emotional aspect.

Implications for Theory

Challenging previous research, the overwhelming majority of men expressed emotional attachment to outside partners. Previous research positioned men as lacking emotional involvement in their affairs and seeking only sexual attachments, while presenting women as emotionally invested in affairs (Banfield & McCabe, 2001; Glass & Wright, 1985; Spanier & Margolis, 1983). Men repeatedly spoke of the emotional benefits of their outside partnerships and the ways those relationships helped address unmet emotional needs. Men sought women who expressed interest in their feelings, opinions, goals, and fears. They resented their wives, whom they perceived as now bored with them and their emotional lives. They believed their outside partnerships to contain emotional intimacy, including the provision of praise and friendship. They also sought relational management.

The role of masculinity in terms of the motivation for outside partnerships and the ways outside partners boosted their sense of themselves challenges commonsense notions of men's motivations in seeking outside partnerships. The men in this study employ participation in outside partnerships as an act of compensatory masculinity to combat their feelings of emasculation. The concept of compensatory masculinity isn't new.

Its use here in examining the dynamics of primary partnerships and outside partnerships represents an expansion of the concept. However, Minjeong Kim (2014) also used compensatory masculinity to explain South Korean husbands in international marriages "emphasis on heterosexual desirability and virility" (Kim, 2014, p. 291). As mentioned previously, Christin Munsch's 2015 study also used compensatory masculinity to explain the dynamics of infidelity. Thus, this work adds to the existing research expanding the use of the concept.

The men in this study highly valued the validation, support, and relational management they gained in outside partnerships. The sexual encounters in these outside partnerships fell into the popular culture term of the "Girlfriend Experience." They valued the sexual events because of the sensuality, enthusiasm, and passion demonstrated by outside partners. They described marital sex lives replete with rushed and impersonal encounters and/or sexless or near sexless marriages. Further, men reported buy-in into the tenets of the need for validation. Specifically, they reported a belief that women hold the power to validate or invalidate their masculinity through her opinion of his sexual prowess.

Again, ultimately these men employed the Infidelity Workaround exercised by women in my previous study (Walker, 2018). This allows the individual to outsource unsatisfying aspects of the primary partnership to a more interested third party while retaining the status of being married, thus avoiding a costly divorce and the pain of upending their lives (and that of their children's).

Future Research

A longitudinal study of men's participation in outside partnerships would demonstrate whether their perceptions, motivations, and impressions change over time. Since data collection ended, a total of five men, whose interviews had concluded previously, reported their marriages were ending. (One man got caught during his interview, and his marriage ended. The other four ended in the time between the end of data collection and today's writing.) The rest of the men in the sample reported a desire to remain married for the duration. While these few men expressed regret at being caught in their outside partnerships, they also expressed tremendous relief. For them, this meant an end to the lying, sneaking, and subterfuge. Two of the men whose primary partnerships ended after the time of our interview wound up with their long-term outside partners in ongoing relationships of assumed permanence (e.g., living together, plans to marry, etc.). The rest simply broached the singles' pool and began dating in search of another long-term partner. (By contrast, in my previous studies with women, no one reported getting caught, and no divorces initiated during data collection. After data collection and analysis, only two women reported that their marriages had ended. In one case, her participation in outside partnerships played a role. In the other case, her participation never came to light. Neither wound up pairing with their outside partners.) A longitudinal inquiry could better expose the patterns around relationship dissolution, and men's intent to remain in their primary partnerships over time. Given that my previous inquiry into women's experiences in outside partnerships revealed that many women reported a desire to consensually open their primary partnerships, a longitudinal study might reveal whether men's primary partners broach the topic as well. Given men's desire for monogamy in their outside partnerships—which makes sense given the motivation for participation for these men—a longitudinal study might reveal whether men change their minds or this insistence impacts their long-term success with maintaining outside partnerships.

Further, this sample proved overwhelmingly White as a function of the recruitment site. Samples gathered online tend to skew White. This study also failed to consider class. We can assume the sample skews upper- to upper-middle class based on the fees required to maintain membership on *Ashley Madison* and the men's reported occupations, which skewed white collar. An inquiry with richer diversity in both race and class may prove beneficial in puzzling out men's experiences with outside partnerships, particularly those sought online. Given the fact that everyone in this study logged onto *Ashley Madison* with the intent of procuring a partner, their experiences are vastly different than people who've fallen into an outside partnership through organic means (e.g. coworkers, neighbors, etc.). Thus, an inquiry looking at men whose outside part-nerships began organically—or even a study comparing the experiences of men in organic outside partnerships versus men in outside partner-ships entered purposefully—might shed more light on men's experiences in outside partnerships.

Conclusions

This sample of men ranged from 27 to 70 years of age, but the average age was 45.9. Men between the ages of 30–49 encompassed more than half of the sample. Only six of the men identified as a person of color. All but one man in the group identified as heterosexual. All but six men were married; those six men described themselves as partnered. All but two of the men wanted to remain in their primary relationships. Most had children. A third of the men reported sexual inexperience prior to entering into marriage. More than two-thirds described sexless primary partnerships. The men in this sample reported much deliberation before making the decision to enter into an outside partnership.

Most of the women with whom I spoke reported that their primary motivation was sexual pleasure and their outside partnerships func-tioned to outsource the sexual facet of their relationships. They spoke of emotionally satisfying primary partnerships. These men spoke of primary partnerships where their perception of a lack of an enthusiastic sexual partner, lack of relational management, and their primary partners' disin-terest in their feelings, fears, and events of their days resulted in a loss of self-esteem. Specifically, the men believed themselves to be "less-than" and emasculated. They internalized the U.S. social narrative stating that their partner's disinterest signals a lack of prowess and skill on their part. For these men, outside partnerships offered opportunities to validate their masculinity via sexual prowess, and it represented a space where a sexual partner lavished attention, praise, and care upon them. For these men, outside partnerships function as acts of compensatory manhood and outside partnerships provide sexual encounters of the Girlfriend Experience variety. These men espoused a need for validation, including the belief that women hold the power to validate and invalidate a man's masculinity through her opinion of his sexual prowess. And men sought outside partners to perform the relational management their primary partners failed to offer. These outside partnerships worked to alleviate the stress of men's experiences of emasculation, and validate their manhood.

Like the women in the previous study, men exercised the Infidelity Workaround, which seeks to outsource unsatisfying aspects of the primary partnership to a more interested third party. Doing so allows the individual to address their unmet needs while retaining the status of being married, avoiding the emotional upset of toppling their current lives, and circumventing the stigma, pain, and expense of a divorce. While the vast majority of the women in my last book sought to outsource the sexual aspect of their primary partnerships, which were relationships where the women reported satisfying emotional connections, a small minority of those women reported primary partnerships lacking emotional closeness and connection. Like those seven women, the men in this study also sought to outsource the emotional aspect of their primary partnerships via sexual outside partnerships.

References

Banfield, S., & McCabe, M. P. (2001). Extra relationship involvement among women: Are they different from men? *Archives of Sexual Behavior, 30*(2), 119–142. https://doi.org/10.1023/A:1002773100507.

Glass, S. P., & Wright, T. L. (1985). Sex differences in type of extramarital involvement and marital dissatisfaction. *Sex Roles, 12,* 1101–1120. https://doi.org/10.1007/BF00288108.

Graham, C. A., Mercer, C. H., Tanton, C., Jones, K. G., Johnson, A. M., Wellings, K., & Mitchell, K. R. (2017). What factors are associated with reporting lacking interest in sex and how do these vary by gender? Findings from the third British national survey of sexual attitudes and lifestyles. *BMJ Open, 7*(9), e016942. https://doi.org/10.1136/bmjopen-2017-016942.

Gunst, A., Ventus, D., Kärnä, A., Salo, P., & Jern, P. (2016). Female sexual function varies over time and is dependent on partner-specific factors: A population-based longitudinal analysis of six sexual function domains. *Psychological Medicine, 47*(2), 1–12. https://doi.org/10.1017/S00332917 16002488.

Kim, M. (2014). South Korean rural husbands, compensatory masculinity, and international marriage. *Journal of Korean Studies, 19*(2), 291–325. https://doi.org/10.1353/jks.2014.0030.

Klusmann, D. (2002). Sexual motivation and duration of partnership. *Archives of Sexual Behavior, 31*(3), 275–287. https://doi.org/10.1023/A:1015205020769.

Klusmann, D. (2006). Sperm competition and female procurement of male resources as explanations for a gender-specific time dependent course in the sexual motivation of couples. *Human Nature, 17*(3), 283–300. https://doi.org/10.1007/s12110-006-1010-2.

Morton, H., & Gorzalka, B. B. (2014). The role of partner novelty in sexual functioning: A Review. *Journal of Sex and Marital Therapy, 41*(6). https://doi.org/10.1080/0092623x.2014.958788.

Sims, K. E., & Meana, M. (2010). Why did passion wane? A qualitative study of married women's attributions for declines in desire. *Journal of Sex and Marital Therapy, 36,* 360–380. https://doi.org/10.1080/0092623X.2010.498727.

Spanier, G. B., & Margolis, R. L. (1983). Marital separation and extramarital sexual behavior. *Journal of Sex Research, 19,* 23–48. https://doi.org/10.1080/00224498309551167.

Thomas, W. I., & Thomas, D. S. (1928). *The child in America: Behavior problems and programs.* New York: Knopf.

Walker, A. M. (2018). *The secret life of the cheating wife: Power, pragmatism, and pleasure in women's infidelity.* Lanham, MD: Lexington Books.

.

Index

Made in the USA
Monee, IL
04 November 2022

17115747R00122